uniforms
or exploit others?

o.

. Okay. And at th
eplica cruiser, a fal
rm. Were you conc
lice officer?

can't see him do –

v: Why not? You st
what

THE FIRST SURVIVOR

THE FIRST SURVIVOR

Life With Canada's Deadliest Mass Shooter

LISA BANFIELD

WITH SHERRI AIKENHEAD

AND MAUREEN BANFIELD

SUTHERLAND HOUSE

TORONTO, 2026

Sutherland House
416 Moore Ave., Suite 304
Toronto, ON M4G 1C9

First edition, January 2026

If you are interested in inviting one of our authors to a live event or media appearance, please contact sarah@sutherlandhousebooks.com and visit our website at sutherlandhousebooks.com for more information.

We acknowledge the support of the Government of Canada.

Manufactured in Canada
Cover designed by Lena Yang
Book composed by Karl Hunt

Cover image courtesy of The Canadian Press, photographer Andrew Vaughan

Endpaper details courtesy of Mass Casualty Commission, Public Hearings Transcript, July 15, 2022, https://masscasualtycommission.ca/files/documents/transcripts/EN_20220715_PublicHearings_Transcript.pdf.

Library and Archives Canada Cataloguing in Publication
Title: The first survivor : life with Canada's deadliest mass shooter / Lisa Banfield ; with Sherri Aikenhead and Maureen Banfield.
Names: Banfield, Lisa, author. | Aikenhead, Sherri, author. | Banfield, Maureen, author.
Identifiers: Canadiana (print) 20250304317 | Canadiana (ebook) 20250304511 | ISBN 9781997701095 (hardcover) | ISBN 9781997701101 (EPUB)
Subjects: LCSH: Banfield, Lisa. | LCSH: Abused wives—Canada—Biography. | LCSH: Wife abuse—Canada. | LCSH: Gender-based violence—Canada. | LCSH: Mass shootings—Nova Scotia. | LCGFT: Autobiographies.
Classification: LCC HV6626.23.C3 B36 2026 | DDC 362.82/92092—dc23

ISBN 978-1-997701-09-5
eBook 978-1-997701-10-1

CONTENTS

AUTHOR'S NOTE

AS I WRITE my story, I struggle to know where to start. I have always been concerned about what others wanted, needed, or perceived. Now I see that my fawning default may have been the perfect pheromone for my ill-fated relationship with Gabriel Wortman. Our nineteenth anniversary, on April 18, 2020, imploded and became the catalyst for a mass murder. Within twenty-four hours, the man I loved killed twenty-two innocent people including an unborn child. My secret life of intimate partner violence culminated in Canada's worst mass shooting. I can't presume to speak for the grieving families whose lives were forever changed that weekend. Their lost loved ones will never be forgotten, and I respectfully honour them.

Strangers who've wondered and written about me may only be interested in learning the facts of that horrific weekend and its aftermath. I've wondered how many are interested in understanding me, the flawed woman who became the groomed victim of a psychopath. Or the naïve girl who believed love and faith were all that mattered in this world. Depending on your position, my life story may not capture your interest or change your presumptive beliefs. My hope is that it touches you in a way that challenges what you think about humanity, class, privilege, power, and influence. My deepest desire is that it inspires compassion and change in how people view women in abusive relationships. Even as I write this book, domestic violence has been declared an epidemic for women in Nova Scotia. Eight unprotected Nova Scotia women died at the hands of their partners in a six-month period between October 2024 and March 2025. In many ways, my story is their story.

PROLOGUE

APRIL 18, 2020

I HEARD REVERBERATING shots through the night—or was it the many fireworks we had stored on our rural Nova Scotia property for celebratory occasions? No. These sounds were ominously unfamiliar. The successive explosions almost stopped my heart as I pushed onward into the woods.

Barefoot, I bolted into the forest, oblivious of the pain as I stumbled over sticks and stumps. I shielded my eyes with my hands from the dense branches. Forced to drop to my hands and knees, I crawled through the backwoods underbrush.

My left hand throbbed from the handcuff I'd ripped off in the backseat of a replica RCMP car, where Gabriel left me as he gathered up guns. I couldn't stop to think about the beating he had just given me on the eve of our nineteenth anniversary, or where he could be now. Every branch that snapped could give me away. I ignored the searing pain in my back, where he'd kicked me onto the floor.

Weary, yet intent on surviving, I finally came upon an uprooted tree trunk large enough to hide me. *Thank you, God.* I prayed as I huddled inside it for warmth and safety. My torn yoga pants and spandex long-sleeve shirt were a meagre buffer between me and the cold earth. I now realized Gabriel was truly capable of murder.

For hours, I buried my nose and mouth into my shirt to conceal my breath from Gabriel's hunting eyes, as the chilling air dipped to zero. April evenings typically brought frost in Nova Scotia, and I was beginning to feel it. I prayed repeatedly that I would survive until morning.

I had no idea that Gabriel killed thirteen innocent people, as I lay trembling in a tree hollow. He stealthily slipped out of our neighbourhood through a blueberry field road before 11:00 p.m., evading police on Portapique Beach Road, which connects to the highway. He would go on to kill nine more people before he was serendipitously stopped.

As the sun rose at about 6:30 a.m., I crawled out to the woods' edge. I crouched down in the ditch and saw a black SUV race down the road. Was Gabriel still out there looking for me? I waited until it passed. This might have been my only chance to get help. I ran as fast as my numb feet could carry me. To my far left, I saw a driveway with a camper trailer next to a grey house. I'd never been here before, but I banged on the door, praying someone would answer. In my panic, I feared Gabriel could still come through the woods at any minute and shoot me.

A dog barked as my heart pounded and my stomach churned. After what seemed like forever, Leon, a neighbour I barely knew, opened the door and stared at me for a second. As he moved the dog aside, I rushed past him.

"Gabriel lost it!" I gasped.

"No shit! He's burned down his own house, Lisa," Leon told me.

"Call 911!"

I looked for a place to get away from the windows in his living room, then ran into his tiny bathroom. I spotted a little window and assessed within seconds that I could climb through it to escape, if Gabriel burst in.

I heard Leon talking to the dispatcher, "I got a guy's wife here and she's freaking out. Can you send a cop to get her? There's a lot of shit up here last night and I don't know what's going on."

He handed me the phone. My hand shook uncontrollably as I tried to hold it to my ear.

"Hi Lisa. We're going to help you, OK. Stay on the phone with me. OK, I'm just talking to the officers. You're not injured, are you?" he asked.

"I'm in pain right now," I cried.

"Where are you hurting?"

"My back, it . . . I'm just—" I couldn't find words and openly cried.

"OK, we're going to get you some help and then we're going to get you some medical attention."

Within minutes, the SWAT team arrived and told me to come out.

I went out onto the deck and froze. Men dressed in camouflage pointed their guns at me. "Come to me," one officer motioned to me. Leon gave me his coat and sneakers. Lurching forward, I reached for the officer's arms. He told me his name was Ben and that he would keep me safe. I didn't believe him. We were in the open and I was terrified that Gabriel would walk out of the woods and kill me for running away.

Shaking and straining to speak, my teeth were rattling beneath my blue, quivering lips. I was hysterical by this time. "Please, let me get in the car," I begged.

"Lisa, I'm over six feet and I have all these armed officers around you. He can't get you. We are waiting for a secure vehicle to transport you."

It seemed so long—although it was likely only minutes—before an RCMP van pulled onto the property. They rushed me first to the end of Portapique Beach Road, where RCMP cars and black SUVs blocked its entrance, then to a nearby fire station in Great Village. They transferred me into an ambulance where they covered me with blankets, trying to stop me from shivering.

The paramedics examined my back injuries, then hooked me up to an IV to give me painkillers that worked quickly. By the time I reached the Colchester East Hants Health Centre, forty kilometres away, my mind had calmed. I felt numb and shell-shocked. I tried to make sense of what had happened the night before: hearing gunshots, explosions, and distant voices with an eerie backdrop of fire and smoke, all the while stifling my own terror.

I had yet to learn the depths of Gabriel's evil as my world fell away. Just seven hours earlier, Gabriel killed thirteen innocent people within an hour of my escape. He had snuck out of our neighbourhood undetected through a blueberry field, evading the police waiting at the entrance to Portapique Beach Road.

* * *

In my hospital bed, my mind chased images of Gabriel: *He is out there somewhere and he is going to kill my family, starting with my sister, Maureen.* Hours later, Maureen walked into my hospital room. We locked eyes, overwhelmingly grateful to see one another alive. Without a word, Maureen's presence allowed me to exhale. We hugged and sobbed.

After years of fearing Gabriel would kill my family, we were all safe. *Despite the reassurances from the RCMP that Gabriel was dead and I had nothing to fear, my nightmare was far from over.*

The RCMP eventually told us there were "casualties," but I would not learn of the tragic murders of innocent neighbours, friends, and strangers until the following day. The thirteen murders grew to twenty-two (including a pregnant woman). None of us would be the same. It would be years before I absorbed the cataclysmic events of April 18 and 19, 2020.

PART I

Who am I?

Life's destiny starts well before you are aware of its existence. And yet, within me, there was always a knowing—no matter what happens, God will take care of me.

1

It Starts and Ends with Family

I TREASURE MEMORIES of my childhood. I never felt alone growing up. My loneliness took hold later. I come from a family of nine kids, three boys and six girls, so leaning on my sisters came naturally to me. Born Lisa Diana on August 27, 1968, I am the second-youngest of my family and would become the most scrutinized.

A stubborn scrapper from early on, I looked a bit like a tomboy and acted like one. I feared nothing. I loved adventure, and Mom said I played for hours, amusing myself contentedly. I remember how much fun I had making mudcakes after a rain shower. Mom said I even ate a few. I sucked my thumb, which left me buck-toothed as a young girl. My earliest memories are of our cozy 900-square-foot house in the small rural community of Beaver Bank, Nova Scotia.

We youngest girls—Maureen, Joan, Janice, and I—slept four to a bed in the faux-panelled, uninsulated basement of our small bungalow. We shared Mom and Dad's old queen mattress, which sagged slightly in the middle. Cuddling side by side, when one of us rolled over in the middle of the night, the rest would follow without complaint. We generated memories that marked rites of passage throughout our childhood. Our sisterhood was cemented by those unifying experiences and we nostalgically lean on those sweet times still today. I think my need to nurture others came from how all my siblings would take care of each other, no matter what.

My role model was my mother, Beulah Mae (née Zinck). I remember so much of her presence, beauty, cheekiness, and fighting spirit. Now more than ever, I see she was the biggest influence in my life. Beulah was born in the seaside village of West Jeddore, Nova Scotia, where she grew up until she moved to Halifax. The daughter of Wellington and Myrtle Zinck, she had three siblings with whom she remained close her entire life. They were a musically talented family, and Beulah was a vivacious and beautiful spirit.

In 1949, she met my father, Gilbert Banfield, at a local community dance. Beulah's brown eyes often communicated what she thought. That night, though, it was her smile that caught Dad's attention. Dancing to swing music, Dad whirled her about, instantly smitten by the curly-haired girl. Although he managed to get her name, she left before he got her telephone number.

The Banfields' origins began in Bay L'Argent, Newfoundland. They moved to Halifax when Dad was a teen. Gilbert John grew up playing baseball and hockey, and as a natural athlete he was scouted for both sports. His greatest love was hockey, and he quickly led the Fairview Aces to many tournament wins. Wherever Gil went, people gravitated toward him. He loved a good party and was often the life of the party making everyone laugh. By the time he met Mom, Gilbert was a tall, strapping six feet, with Paul Newman's chiseled face and blue eyes. He liked to drink beer and tell stories.

Several weeks after the community dance, my father and his buddies drove to Sir Sandford Fleming Park, a large, forested park on Halifax Northwest Arm, where families swam in frigid waters. "The Dingle," as it was known, appealed to the young and old as a great gathering spot, especially on weekends. A ten-storey stone Memorial

Tower off Dingle Road drew kids to hike up the circular iron steps and hang out the window at the top, overlooking one of Halifax's most incredible views. Gilbert looked out the passenger door of his buddy's truck as they drove on the road circling the tower. He hollered at his buddy: "Stop, stop. That's Beulah." He hopped out of the truck and raced up the narrow, circular stairwell, out of breath as he surprised Mom on the top deck. It took just a few dates before Mom promised Dad, "I'll have as many babies as you want." And she did.

Mom often shared stories of their courtship with us girls, and it was clear they were in love from the get-go. Soon after they met, they got married. Over the course of their fifty-eight years of marriage, Beulah gave birth to nine children. Gil earned decent pay as a linesman for the Maritime Telegraph and Telephone company (MT&T), which allowed them to rent a small home in Fairview. It was here, they began growing their family. Charles was born in 1950, the same year they married. They endured three miscarriages in short succession after Mom had Beverley. Even after the doctor told Mom she would not be able to have any more children, Beulah delivered Jimmy, Dougie, and Brenda. Six years later, she had Maureen, who became our second mother. Then came Joan, whom I idolized, me, and finally Janice, who had a feistiness about her as the youngest and most protected. Even today, we all share a remarkable bond that I consider a precious gift from God.

By the time I came along, the eldest, Charles, was eighteen and my five older siblings had formed their own connection. My parents had saved enough money to put a down payment on their own home in a more rural, affordable area, Beaver Bank, a half an hour from the city limits. In some ways, we were two families under one roof—but not for very long, as my older brothers and sisters moved out before their twenties. Growing up, the Banfield clan must have looked to our neighbours like the *Beverly Hillbillies* we watched on TV. We trucked up Quarry Road, owned by Barrett's Lumber Company that operated practically outside our door. Neighbours sensed we were different, but in an intriguing way. Our close-knit family sparked in others a curiosity: How could we get along so well with that many people in a small home? They often joke that we could form our own baseball team.

They watched us embrace nature by expanding our backyard into the backwoods. We took over a field that later became our pick-up baseball diamond. Neighbourhood kids joined us, playing all day until our moms yelled for us to come for supper. In those days, we picked our teams by tossing the bat back and forth. The person to get the top knob won first pick. We experienced the greatest sense of community during summer breaks. The friendships we formed then remain constant, yet it was my siblings who always had my back.

Money was always tight. Dad often said, "Money doesn't grow on trees." I never felt poor growing up, even though we wore plastic Ben's Bread bags on our feet within our old leaky rubber boots. We looked forward to getting our *new* clothes from hand-me-downs of siblings and others. We didn't get the popular toys our friends owned. When someone up the road got a Lemon Twist—the newest Easter toy that you put on your ankle and twirl in a circle, jumping over the plastic lemon like your very own skip rope—we created our own version. Maureen tied a long rope to an empty paint can and told us to jump when she whipped it in a circle around us. We didn't have Easter baskets or bonnets. Instead, our parents filled our well-worn winter hats with chocolate and a skipping rope with that brand-new sweet smell.

My mom was the powerhouse manager of our home who made ends meet. Like many women of the '70s, her life revolved around the clock on our kitchen wall. While we slept, she baked bread at 4:30 a.m. as part of her days dedicated to cooking and cleaning. Mom prepared a sandwich, apple, and if we were lucky a wagon wheel chocolate cookie. She lined up our brown paper lunch bags on the counter with our names written on them—oldest to youngest. We'd scoff down our homemade breakfast meal of doughboys (fried bread dough), or Quaker's oatmeal, and she'd send us off with a quick kiss: "Have fun and be good." I can only imagine the welcomed silence as the last one of us closed the screen door.

Once safely down the road and out of sight to catch our school bus, Mom did her chores for the day. She did the laundry with a scrub board and steel bucket. By the time I was in junior high, she had upgraded to the prized wringer washer. It not only saved her time but relieved the pain of her arthritis. She was able to quickly hang them to dry on the clothes line that Dad hung the length of our yard. Mom loved the smell of freshly blown laundry. She was an incredible multitasker, prepping every meal while keeping the house clean and tidy for Dad's return.

When we hopped off the school bus, I ran up the hill trying to be the first through the door to see what was for supper. Some days we could smell the distinctive odor of roast chicken or my favourite, her deep-fried, home-cut potatoes. I would run all the faster when that scent wafted through the air, open the screen door with excitement, and yell, "I'm first." Mom served us as we came through the door like a seasoned short-order cook.

If she made barley soup or baked beans, I turned up my nose and stomped downstairs. I knew I'd have to eat it or go to bed hungry. I have always been a picky eater; even today, I don't like trying anything new. Sometimes I went too far, complaining to Mom, "We're having that crap?" "Crap" was as close to a swear word I could use without getting the strap.

"There are kids in the world that don't get to eat at all, so you should be grateful."

Of course, I knew she was right and felt bad after I'd said it. Especially when I thought about how hard Mom worked. She always made us feel extra special on our birthdays by making our favorite homemade chocolate birthday cake with boiled icing. I was too young to appreciate all her sacrifices for us.

While Mom kept the house running, Maureen entertained us younger sisters throughout our childhood. As the oldest of the four younger girls, she helped fill our days with inventive play as our teacher, event planner, entertainment guide, and protector; she would later become my rock. She turned our basement and backwoods into places where our imagination flourished, and our small world grew bigger. Where else could we be Swiss Family Robinson survivors? She invented games based on what we watched on our black-and-white, floor-model TV. In Maureen's version of *The Price Is Right*, she lined us up on the kitchen counter and called for us to "come on down." We also pretended to be Holly Hobbie restaurateurs, lawyers in a courtroom, athletes training for gymnastic competitions, and *Little House on the Prairie* settlers making our own teepee home out of fir tree branches.

Sundays were the best. We would prepare all day for an evening talent show for Mom and Dad. We'd make up funny skits, practice songs, then giggle, and argue as we rehearsed for hours. This tradition provided respite for Mom and Dad from the long work week, especially for Mom, whose work was never done.

Like other dads of that era, he was the stern disciplinarian who would even bring out the belt if needed. One night when Mom and Dad got home from a dance, they discovered icing from the cake Mom made earlier partially eaten. None of us would admit to it, so a frustrated Dad said, "Oh, the ghost is back." We thought we were off the hook, so we rushed to bed. Just then Dad popped his head in our bedroom door, "Not saying your prayers, eh?"

Joan and I immediately dropped to our knees to say our prayers. I looked up at the door and he was now standing there holding a leather belt.

"Put out your hand," he insisted.

I put mine out first and he said, "No, Joan is first." I watched him strike her palm while dreading my turn. The belt stung my palm and wrist and instantly welted. Following our punishment, he'd always say, "You know I love you, right?" It was just his way—and yet, as a kid, I thought if you loved me, you wouldn't hit me.

As the baby, Janice got away with a lot more. Sometimes she'd take the blame for our misdeeds, so we didn't get strapped. We later learned Dad didn't strap Janice as much as we thought. I think he was getting older and softened by the time his baby girl was born. Besides, after all these years, the fear of the belt was an effective deterrent.

We witnessed true love between Mom and Dad growing up and aside from us getting the belt, we never saw any violence. They would laugh, flirt, and loved to dance. On weekdays, while we watched our favourite soap opera, *Another World*, Mom prepared herself for Dad's arrival from work. She'd slip into the tiny bathroom and emerge in a flowered mini dress with freshly sprayed Cachet perfume. Her hair was perfectly coiffed from the day's setting of tight pin curls, and she wore crimson ruby lipstick that framed her naturally full lips. I could feel her excitement as she greeted Dad at the door with a hug and kiss. This ritual stuck with me. I learned at an early age a woman's worth and value depended on how she looked and treated her man.

Mom's catering to Dad's every want and need, including preparing his meals and delivering them on a TV tray to the living room, left an imprint on my feminine core. In fact, the selfless way she tended to all of us modeled for me how to show love. Like Mom, serving others gave me purpose. Yet over the years, I saw her passion turn to exhaustion, sadness, resentment, and eventually, addiction.

For his part, my father instilled in me a strong faith that came from a God-fearing upbringing. While Mom grew up Baptist, she didn't practice this faith or attend church beyond the ceremonial traditions.

We were raised Anglican. Dad read the Bible most nights. These readings formed the basis of our family's code. He would remind us, "Do unto others as you would have done to you." On Sundays, Dad took us to the St. John's Anglican Church while Mom stayed home to cook dinner. As a young child, I developed my own relationship with God and to this day, find great solace in my daily prayers.

We often competed for Dad's approval and affection. One time, I tried to stand out as his special daughter by mowing the lawn before he got home from work. I stood in the driveway, my hands on the gas-powered mower, waiting for him to pull in the yard with his two-tone cream-and-orange Ford truck. I felt grown up, grinning with pride, as I had spared him from the yard work. But I could tell from his reaction, my job wasn't up to snuff. "Thanks, hon, but you didn't mow the rows properly," he said, minimizing my effort. His standards were high. Even when I bought him a present with my own money from a paper route or babysitting, he'd say, "I don't need this; give it to someone who needs it more." Not that he was unappreciative, but that's the way he thought. Regardless, it left me feeling unworthy and never good enough.

I was skinny and scrawny, so my siblings affectionately nicknamed me "Boy." It hurt my feelings but if I showed it, they would only tease me more. As a sensitive kid, I wanted to do as well as my sisters in school. But I struggled so much with math that I would fake being sick during test days. It got worse when Dad tried to help by sitting me down at the kitchen table, got out the math book and attempted to teach me long-division his way. He would keep me there for hours without a break. Dad was a perfectionist and when I didn't print "4" the way he wanted, he'd erase it and make me do it over. His voice got louder with his increased frustration level. Despite his methods, I knew he cared and really wanted to help me. We spent so much time together that year, but not in the way I wanted.

I ended up failing Grade 4. All my sisters were good students and passed with what seemed like minimal effort. Academics, especially math, left me feeling stupid. I couldn't understand why I wasn't as smart as them. It made me more insecure and chipped away at my self-esteem. The only good thing that came of being kept back a year was being able to hang out with my kid sister Janice, who became my best friend. Born with a sparkle in her eyes, Janice had an engaging spirit like Mom. She was unfiltered and had no problem socially, fitting in anywhere. I attended summer school for math and luckily moved on to Sackville Heights Junior High. Janice and I remained in the same grade until we graduated from Millwood High in 1988. These school troubles weighed on me even in my adulthood, an insecurity my future partner would later use to belittle and demean me.

2

I Don't Matter

ALTHOUGH MATH WAS always tough for me, I developed a love of writing. In my preteen years, Joan bought me my own diary with a mini lock. Through journaling, I finally found a safe place to express my feelings without judgment. On those pages, I was strong and confident. No one could criticize me. I never revisited those passages until four decades later, when I finally looked back on what had happened during my life. Many of my adolescent journals were safely stored in my family home, but most of the ones written during my relationship were later destroyed by fire. It was interesting to look back—and also troublesome. I remember distinctly when my life changed, and it was long before I met Gabriel.

My innocence abruptly ended when I was fourteen years old.

* * *

Our large family ran on a tight budget, so as my older siblings got jobs, they had to contribute to the household. Maureen earned her spending money by babysitting, then began working part-time in Downsview Mall throughout high school. As soon as I became a teenager, I also got to babysit and loved looking after the little ones.

I felt like an adult even though I was gullible, young, and naive as a teenager.

With my earnings, I got my first purse. It was exciting to earn my own money to buy things I wanted. There were lots of local families with children, so babysitting seemed an ideal job opportunity for someone underage. When Maureen got a real job at the local mall, I got to take over her babysitting gigs. Some nights I slept overnight, especially when the parents arrived home late. It was easier to walk home in the morning. I got five dollars an hour, and felt like a millionaire—until the night I was molested by the father of the kids I babysat.

I knew what he'd done was wrong, but he was a trusted adult. I felt so embarrassed. I told no one, not even my sisters. I ended up babysitting again, but pretended to be sleeping while lying on my stomach so he couldn't touch me. It didn't matter; he kept doing it. I needed the money so I continued to babysit.

One night Mom, Maureen, and I were playing cards at the kitchen table when the phone rang. I answered and was asked to babysit for the same family. "I'll babysit but I want to come home afterwards. I'm not staying overnight," I blurted emphatically.

Maureen grabbed my arm and pulled me into the bathroom. The medicine cabinet mirror above the pink pedestal sink reflected my flushed face. She knew. "He's doing it to you, isn't he?" she said, enraged. I knew at that moment Maureen had been molested by him, too.

Our sisterly bond forged another layer through that joint traumatic experience. Maureen pushed open the bathroom door and confronted Mom. "I told you it would happen again!"

Her loud voice alarmed Dad, who came out of the bedroom. He asked what was going on.

I worked up the nerve to tell what had been happening, but his response confused me.

"Is that all?" he said, looking at me as if what a married man did to his baby girl was OK.

As I walked away, I believed for the first time in my life that I didn't matter. That what happened to me was OK. My parents, my most cherished guardians, didn't protect me.

I would never be the same.

Afterwards, Maureen and I shared a deep-seated shame and blame. Our reality was discounted and ignored. Our parents and others acted as if the molestation didn't happen. Back in the day, things like this weren't talked about. That left us feeling unworthy of the protection and love that we sought and needed. Maureen later said, "Lisa's light dimmed, and I felt her insecurities and anxiousness grow."

After that, the dynamic in our house changed. Janice knew something was going on by the way I was acting. Boldly, she went to Mom and confronted her. "What's going on with Lisa?" she demanded.

"Go talk to your father." Mom avoided the uncomfortable. She deferred to Dad whenever she felt out of her depth. Janice asked Dad directly, "What happened?"

He blew it off and shockingly allowed Janice to babysit for them again. But Janice was ballsy. Unlike me, she had conviction at an early age that emboldened her. She not only wanted to babysit, but she was ready to confront him.

Janice told us what happened: "I laid on the floor by the beds where his kids were sleeping. I stayed quietly awake until they arrived home. Shortly after, I heard the door creak open, and he walked in. I didn't close my eyes. He crept over to me and kneeled beside me. I sat up sharply, 'What are you doing?'"

Stunned and without a word, the molester stood up and left the bedroom. It never happened again while she babysat. I was so proud of her, but I felt inferior; as her older sister, I couldn't do what she had so bravely done. Neither did Maureen.

From then on, I never wandered too far from home and felt lonelier than ever. I had one friend at school. When she moved, I had to find another friend so I wouldn't be alone between classes. That's when I met Denise. She became my bestie and, outside of my sisters, the one person I trust in this world. She remains my best friend to this day.

"Lisa was super shy but I liked her," recalled Denise. Although we didn't live close to each other, we hung out at school and talked over the phone a lot. I wanted to invite her to stay one weekend, but I was worried about what she would think of my family. Denise only had a couple of siblings, so I was thrilled she agreed to a sleepover. She was the only friend I ever invited for a sleepover.

Denise shared, "I met her mom and thought, this woman is fantastic. She baked us treats. Her mom was a doll. They said, 'I love you a lot,' to one another. I'm like, what? Their open affection and down-to-earth friendliness made me feel at ease."

But the Banfield house was far from ideal. While Mom and Dad shared a love story, life was filled with behind-closed-door realities. Dad was an alcoholic. Financial hardships led to arguments and a steady undercurrent of tension. Eventually, Dad was charged with driving under the influence. He lost his driver's license and had to retire from MT&T after thirty-five years of service. Committed to providing for those of us still living at home, he found another job at the Halifax Dockyard as a stevedore.

Some days, Mom would be left at home from early morning until late at night. She was lonely and eventually drank every night, too. One night, sleeping in our basement bedroom, we awoke to the familiar sound of the wrestling keys after one of Dad's benders. We'd listen to his muted mutterings and a chair scuffing the floor as he tried to sit down to remove his heavy, steel-toed work boots. My parents argued and their voices rose. Maureen would try to comfort us by covering our ears and singing softly to us until the yelling subsided.

Once, I had to pick up Dad from the Load of Mischief, the neighbourhood bar where he spent time with his friends. With Denise, I jumped in the Pinto we jokingly referred to as the Green Hornet, and off we went. She stayed in the backseat while I went inside, praying that Dad wasn't in the stripper section of the bar. "If he's in there, I'm gonna be mad," I said to Denise.

Even though I was too young to be in the bar, the local hangout's rules were quite lax. Dad was the "Norm" of the place and, like in *Cheers*, everyone knew his name. Unfazed, he introduced me to all of his buddies.

Sharing so many memories like this with Denise drew us closer. "Lisa seemed innocent, cautious, and even nervous. When she did go out, she had so much fun but was always the designated driver. The guys flocked after her. They were like '*Lisa Banfield*'—they thought she was so attractive in high school," Denise later remembered.

As much as I wanted to be a teenager and hang out at Burger King with my friends, I stayed home to keep Mom company, because Dad would always be out. I've always tried to overlook the faults of those I love, so my father's addiction didn't bother me as much as when Mom started to drink more heavily. She'd quickly stutter and stumble down the hall after getting a top-up of either rum and Coke, or beer. I knew my mother's pain was born out of loneliness, something I experienced as an adolescent.

Our family changed when the oldest siblings moved out. My oldest brother blossomed as a referee in the NHL, and Maureen left at eighteen to marry and pursue a teaching career. I felt lost without her, but was proud she became the first and only Banfield to attend university. That left Joan, Janice, and me at home. As the next in line, Joan moved upstairs to the main floor, second bedroom.

Some nights, while Dad was out, Mom bribed Janice and me to stay home with her. "She would give us special treats like chocolate bars and chips," remembered Janice. As the youngest of nine, Janice always seemed wiser than her years. "We know our parents loved us, but for us four youngest siblings, it was hard to feel special. We developed a sense of unworthiness; outside of us sisters, love seems conditional," recalled Janice.

Janice's personality as a *Snow White* beauty made her popular among her peers, so she was rarely home. I was always tethered to my mother. Not because I had a need to be but because she needed me to be. My siblings sought opportunities to escape from our parents' drinking. They seemed to be able to leave free from guilt; I could not. I registered the forsaken hurt and sadness in Mom's eyes begging me not to go. She screamed without words, *Don't leave me, too,* and I felt compelled to listen. I was unable to deafen her pleas with my own desires or needs. I became so attuned to her pain that relieving it drove me to the shadows. I became a soulless giver.

Denise noticed how torn I became and tried to spend more time with me. She'd bought us tickets to see the Beach Boys in downtown Halifax.

Denise remembered, "It was raining, and time was running out for us to get to the concert on time. I went to the pay phone at the bus terminal and called her, 'Lisa, it's getting late. Where are you?' She told me she couldn't leave her mom alone. I thought it was really unfair. She should be doing the same things as Janice. As much as I loved her mom, it was odd."

People cared for me, but I struggled to accept help or a genuine compliment. I felt embarrassed in some way. It really didn't matter if they were strangers or family; other people's opinions of me reigned in my world.

Then I met my first boyfriend, and everyone else mattered a whole lot less.

3

Love and Faith

LOOKING BACK, I realize my first boyfriend, David, was my saviour. I needed to escape my tether to Mom so when David gave me his undivided attention, for the first time, I felt free. He was the reason I left home.

Taller than my five-foot-five height, he had dark curly hair and captivating blue eyes. I'd never felt anything like it. David's confidence and strength made me light-headed and euphoric. With my Grade 12 diploma in hand, and a new job as a file clerk at a local bank, I felt confident we could make a nice home in one of the apartments his father owned nearby.

Denise dated David's cousin, so it was a double win. We all got to hang out. She wasn't surprised I moved in with him after high school.

"It seemed like we were in such a rush to grow up. Post-secondary or work, we thought, *what now?*" Denise said, looking back.

I loved David deeply. For a couple of years, I was the happiest I'd ever been in my life. I never had big aspirations like many of my peers. I wanted a simple, traditional life: a good husband, a decent-paying job, and a family of my own. I craved unconditional love and hoped to find that in my future partner. My need to please became a near-obsession. Perhaps this obsession added to David's distance. I noticed him drifting and my self-doubt crept in. I felt unworthy of him. My neediness grew, and I think it was too much for him.

On my twentieth birthday, August 27, our relationship ended.

"Don't leave me," I begged.

He walked out and this time, he didn't want to get back together.

Denise tried to help me through it when she saw my overreaction. "It was her first real love and boyfriend. She was so upset," Denise shared.

Still, I thought I could repair things. I constantly drove by his mom's home with Denise, just to get a glimpse of him. Maureen, who was married by now, also tried to help me as I spun out of control. "Your first break-up is crushing, but it is not the end of the world," she told me, trying to talk me down. "I get it. You two will always have a special connection, but Lisa, this is not normal. You have to let it go."

I moved back home to Quarry Road, a place I thought I'd left for good. My return to our family home coincided with the severe illness of my kindred spirit, my sister, Joan. I idolized her. She was only one year older, but Joan had it all. She was glamorous and wore her dark hair in such a fashionable style. Earlier as teens, the two of us snuck off to our bedroom, where we'd laugh as Joan learned to play guitar on an old Yamaha that our cousin gave her. She fantasized about becoming a music star. Mom's relatives on her side of the family were naturally talented musicians who played old country tunes at family kitchen parties. Joan sang in our bedroom while I mimicked her, but her vocal gifts far exceeded mine.

With Joan, I could relax and truly be myself. She tried to teach me how to play guitar, but I never had the patience to build up the calluses on my fingers. That didn't matter, as I loved listening to and watching Joan do anything: her hair, her make-up. We would dress up together and head to the local Corral Pub and Grill in Lower

Sackville's Downsview Mall. Sometimes Joan would join the band on stage to sing a tune or two. Even though I wasn't up there with her, I felt just as special because she was my sister.

Like me, Joan was in and out of our childhood home but when she became ill, she moved back home permanently. At age nineteen, she was diagnosed with acute porphyria. Joan inherited a rare blood disease that interrupted her life; she became increasingly weak and couldn't work. The disease made her a candidate for experimental treatments.

I felt her life spirit disappearing as her vitality diminished over the next several years. Joan's body ached with so much pain that she could no longer hold her guitar or do the things she truly loved. Now, to pass time, she started smoking and played cards with Mom at the kitchen table. We should have been out bar-hopping like other twentysome-things. I tried everything to get her out of bed for some fresh air, desperately wanting her to fight on.

JOURNAL ENTRY: APRIL 10, 1992:

Joan, make yourself get out of bed each morning even if it is to go to the living room or down the road for a walk, anything to make yourself more aware of life. You've got to build your strength up Joan, I know you can. You've always been there for me growing up, guiding me, you mean more to me than I can ever express. I just don't want anything bad to happen to you because if you weren't there to hug me when I need a hug, or laugh with me when I'm down, a part of me would die. I'm here if you need a shoulder to cry on or someone to yell at but I won't let you give up! I won't! Love ya Sis, Lisa xo

I remember the day I understood how sick she had become.

"How about a walk?" I suggested. "It's beautiful out."

"I can't. I'm too weak. I can't move."

Frustrated and thinking she was just being lazy, I urged her to come with me.

"Come on, Joan. Get up. I'll help you."

Her silent tears said it all; she seriously couldn't move. That's when I knew something was wrong. I yelled to Mom.

Joan was admitted to the hospital that day. For the next several years, she was in and out of the hospital many times with acute episodes. Doctors pumped her with steroids, and I became more frightened when Joan's body ballooned, and her mental state deteriorated. She was not herself. She struggled to pretend she was OK.

By spring 1993, Joan entered the hospital for the last time. I comforted her in any way I could, trying to rekindle her incredible laugh. Her paralysis prevented her from even scratching her face. My most tender moments with her came during the last few weeks of her life. I crawled up on her bed to brush her hair or wipe her tears as her young body shut down. I caressed her arm while we reminisced about our childhood. We laughed, cried, and whispered prayers of love and comfort. "Pachelbel's Canon" played softly in the background, its lullaby cadence cradling our collective souls.

Our family gathered around her bed and sang, "You Are My Sunshine." She died at age twenty-six on April 14, 1993, leaving our close-knit family deeply traumatized. For the first time in all our lives, one of our siblings was gone.

On a gloomy Saturday, we held her funeral at our childhood St. John's Anglican Church. I drove home while praying for a sign that Joan was OK. Once home, I headed straight to the bedroom while my family sat at the kitchen table talking. The radio played Casey Kasem's *Top 10 Hits* in the background. Because Joan and I were so close, both in age and the way sisters can be, my family worried how I would pull through such a tragic loss.

"Is Lisa going to be OK?" my brothers asked. The numbing grief I felt at that time could have easily swallowed me for years, had it not been for my faith. I prayed as I laid on my bed, "Please give me a sign Lord that I will be OK." Just then Joan's blue eyes appeared to me as she kissed my forehead. At that moment, I knew she was OK, and I would be OK, too. As painful as it felt losing my sister, God would take care of me and help me survive.

A year after Joan's death, my sisters urged me to get out and unwind. At twenty-six, I remained optimistic that I would find my person. My niece Stephanie was like another sister to me. Just four years apart, we often hung out together. One night, we tried out a new country bar. A tall, cute guy with dimples approached me. We struck up a conversation. I couldn't stop looking at his face. He made me laugh. For the first time, I gave a guy my phone number.

I seemed so happy then. I wore my long brown hair in curls down to my shoulders. The way he looked at me made me feel seen. Over the next few months, I fell in love. In some ways, he reminded me of Dad because he loved to hunt and fish, and was an overall good guy. My family, and especially Dad, all approved when we got engaged later that year.

The sun shone on the day I got married, July 5, 1997. My long, white wedding train flowed behind me as Janice, Maureen, and Stephanie stood for me. At twenty-nine, I thought I'd found my life-long soul mate. We both worked, which enabled us to buy a home in Beaver Bank across the street from one of my older sisters. Sadly, it didn't take long to realize that we weren't meant for each other. I always said I would marry a guy like Dad, and I did. Unfortunately, my husband drank. I felt myself aging and yearned to start a family. However, feeling alone in the marriage, I couldn't imagine bringing kids into it. If this is what it's like in our late twenties, what would life be like in our forties? After less than three years of marriage, we separated.

4

The Perfect Guy

AT THIRTY-TWO, I had been separated for several years, and my divorce would soon go through. I moved in with Maureen when she suggested I get back out there. “Let’s go dancing. It will do you good,” she urged me. “You don’t need to jump into anything; just ease your way out of the house.”

Looking back, I don’t think I was ready for a relationship. For the past year, I had lamented my failed marriage. Depressed, I preferred to be by myself, but my family wanted me to meet people. When Maureen suggested we go out for a few hours to a nightclub, I finally agreed to go dancing.

We headed downtown to one of Halifax’s popular hangouts for thirtysomethings where you could dance and listen to local bands. Our table on the upper level overlooked the dance floor. It was a perfect spot for singles wanting to inconspicuously scout the room. Near the entrance, a long bar with high stools and a full wall of liquor in front of a mirror reflected the entire room. It felt great to be out and people-watch. A tall, attractive man standing near the bar caught my eye. I consumed some “liquid courage” and took to the dance floor. I forgot how much I loved to dance, and the music was great. Tunes like Van Morrison’s “Brown Eyed Girl” and other feel-good songs kept us up there until we needed a drink.

Time flew by as we danced for hours. I appreciated getting out. It was time to move on. When we got ready to leave, the fair-haired and distinguished man approached me.

Gabriel Wortman didn't look at all like the dark-haired, rugged men that I typically found attractive. At six-foot-three, he hovered over me, and his twinkling bluish green eyes made my breath flutter. Maureen joked: "He's not your type." But there was something about his charm that kept us talking. For the first time since my husband, I gave out my phone number in hopes he would call me.

As we drove across the bridge that spans Halifax Harbour, Maureen and I reminisced about our night. Maureen suddenly remembered she'd left her credit card at the bar, so we turned around to get it.

When I walked in, Gabriel was still there and swiftly made his way to the bar. "Oh, you're back?" he almost giggled with excitement to see me again.

"Oh no, I'm not staying. My sister is waiting in the car. She forgot her credit card."

"Well, can I call you later when you get home?"

I agreed. As soon as we got home, the phone rang. Gabriel and I talked until 3 a.m. He asked me out for a date that week. I confessed to my sisters that I didn't know how to act; it had been so long. My nerves took over and I began to regret saying yes. "It's time you met people," Maureen tried to reassure me. "Just go out and have fun."

When Gabriel showed up in his BMW convertible and mounted the steps with two dozen long-stemmed red roses, I should have been impressed. Instead, I wanted to back out. This was too showy for me. I wasn't used to being wooed in that way. He also looked different; his hair was much lighter than I remembered. There was nothing I could do now; he was here. I quickly introduced him to Maureen, and we left for our date.

Driving to Halifax, he suggested we go to the Economy Shoe Shop for supper, an iconic bistro known for its social vibe and a unique retro atmosphere. We were in the middle of downtown at a three-way stop sign, when a van rear-ended us. Gabriel made sure I was OK, then got out of the car to speak with the driver. I thought to myself, *Now I'll see what this guy is like because my ex-husband would have freaked out.*

The young girl who hit us was distraught. He told her not to worry. His gentle, caring manner instantly impressed me. He seemed more concerned about her and not at all upset about the minimal damage to his brand-new car. They exchanged information and we continued our date. I initially thought he was phony, with his fancy car and arm full of roses, but the way he handled this situation with grace and calmness made me instantly drop my defences.

After that, our relationship took off. We were the same age, liked the same music, and had the same work ethic. Gabriel owned two denture clinics. He was clearly a go-getter and made things happen. I liked that he was driven and successful. We loved spending time together, and that made me feel special. He made me his priority, and I wasn't used to that. He surprised me with thoughtful gifts and messages all the time. He seemed like the perfect guy.

I had been so lonely in my marriage that to have someone who cared for me and wanted to do things together made me feel wanted and unconditionally loved. I welcomed a fresh start with who I thought was the man of my dreams. Finally, I was happy. I wrote in my journal.

APRIL 21, 2001:

I feel so happy inside. I met this sweet, adorable man who lights my insides like no one has ever done before. I know it's only been three days but yet I feel at home with him.

5 things I'm most grateful for are:

1) *I'm most grateful that you Lord has let me meet such a wonderful man, named Gabriel*
2) *I'm so grateful to have the chance to realize there is more out there as far as a man is concerned*
3) *I'm so grateful for this very moment*
4) *I'm so grateful for this feeling that I feel inside when I think of Gabriel*
5) *I'm grateful for all of my experiences in my life, good and bad, because it has molded me into the person I am today.*

At first, I was insecure about the differences in our education levels. I had only graduated high school and Gabriel had attended university, where he studied business and psychology. While Gabriel's intelligence attracted me, it also made me feel inferior, even unworthy of the pedestal he put me on.

"I met this guy," I told my best friend Denise. "He's not my type but I really like him."

Denise was living a full life of her own. We saw little of each other at that time but maintained our friendship by talking over the phone when we could. I was happy when Denise finally got to meet Gabriel. Denise knew me better than most, so she understood why I fell for this guy. "Gabriel was charming and intelligent. I always thought it was the intelligence she was drawn to. He was superior in his knowledge and presence," Denise said, looking back at that time.

I moved in with Gabriel within three months of our first date. Before settling in Dartmouth, Gabriel worked as a funeral director in New Brunswick. He told me he even worked as an embalmer, but he wanted a career as a denturist. He opened the business after graduating from a denturist program. He turned the bottom floor of his Dartmouth house into the Atlantic Denture Clinic. The entrance faced a busy main street. He encouraged me to make the two-storey house our home.

We both liked clean, unique spaces. Gabriel had already started renovating the kitchen and modernizing it. He was creative and inventive and loved building things. I enjoyed redesigning the upstairs rooms and bringing them to life. Between his vision and my touches, it became our home. He'd call me his "Energizer bunny" and commented on how hard I worked. It was exciting and rewarding to have formed a partnership so early in our relationship.

During that first year, it felt like a honeymoon, as we showed each other only the best of ourselves. The way he held me and told me how much he loved me: "I'm so lucky to have you," he kept saying. I was grateful to have found him.

Gabriel was an only child. He grew up in Moncton, New Brunswick, with his parents. He didn't yet know he had a younger brother who had been put up for adoption. He learned that much later in our relationship, when they finally met. He openly shared everything with me.

I asked about his past as we traded stories of our first marriages. He admitted to me that he and his wife had split after seven years because he had cheated on her. He didn't seem that type. He said they weren't happy, and they weren't meant to be. He was not proud of what he did. Though I'd never cheat on my partner, I totally understood marrying the wrong person. I'd done it myself.

We both got so much comfort cuddling and laying together, watching movies. Our intimacy was strong and his desire for me helped me overcome my inhibitions. But when it was time for sleep, his snoring kept me up all night. After weeks of trying to get used to it, I finally told him I couldn't handle it anymore. I woke up too exhausted. He understood. We joked about it after I recorded him. So we turned one of the spare rooms into my little sanctuary. I could still hear him through the walls of the bedroom, but it was an improvement.

As we got closer and more serious, I wanted him to get to know my family and friends. At his first social with the family, you could sense his normal nervousness. We attended a potluck BBQ where everyone mingled. I stayed by his side as I casually introduced him to small groups. He clicked with Maureen's partner—a promising sign since we were so close. Overall, everyone had a good time. They were happy for me and said he seemed nice. Initially, I noticed he would drink more so he could relax, but it soon became obvious that Gabriel was socially awkward, especially as we attended more family gatherings. He'd come up with excuses not to go, or come begrudgingly and insist we leave shortly after arriving. I knew our family could be a lot, so I tried to be patient.

My family began to think he was odd. Gabriel's discomfort worsened. I didn't want to force it. I gave up trying to plan time together with my family. They just didn't get how great he made me feel. Besides, he loved having me to himself. I didn't notice how easily I conceded to his wants and needs. He became increasingly demanding of my time and wanted my undivided attention. My fawning instincts kicked in, and I talked less about my family to appease him because I avoided conflict at all costs. I also just wanted to please him, so I praised him, showed him affection, and threw myself into making our relationship stronger.

I always showed my love through my nurturing side, baking special meals, getting him a beer, or giving him a massage. I loved making him feel as special as he made me feel. I didn't have a problem with it, but Janice would compare me to Edith Bunker, the iconic character from the '70s sitcom *All in the Family*. "I think he can do that for himself," she often remarked. My sisters didn't like how I would dote on him.

Being with Gabriel so much, I found myself missing my family. Maureen noticed it, too. We tried to squeeze in breakfast on Saturdays or go for a walk, but those opportunities decreased. Looking back,

Maureen remembered how she missed me those first six months, but felt reassured by how happy I seemed.

By now I was living a very different life than I had known. As a hairdresser and a bank teller, I had led a modest life. Gabriel showed his love through material things. Gifts of clothing, perfume, jewellery, skin care—anything I showed interest in, he'd buy for me without hesitation. I felt like a princess. Though I contributed to our life together as much as I could, the stress of finances lifted as Gabriel generously supported many of our travel adventures, including road trips to the United States, cruises that I had only ever dreamed of, and trips to the Caribbean. Gabriel obsessively shopped and would buy whatever he wanted. He once surprised me with a diamond ring.

Rereading my journal entry reminds me how hopeful I was.

APRIL 21, 2001:

He is such a very handsome man. But yet has a boyish aura about him. I can tell he has pain within himself too. I hope and pray that we can become the best of friends first . . . I just feel so happy and anxious when I think about him. I hope and pray that he doesn't end up being someone who seems to be such a perfect person for me and then turns out to be another type.

The truth is, in my mid-thirties, I wanted it all: a marriage and children. Gabriel told me early on that he didn't want children. I hoped that maybe in time he would change his mind. Gabriel told me his mother said kids are the worst thing for a marriage. She told him she knew, when she gave birth to him, it was "a mistake." How cruel for a mother to say that to her child! I wanted to understand better, as I had yearned for a family, having grown up with so many siblings. When he had too many drinks, he blamed his parents and how he was raised. He confided he'd been emotionally and physically abused as a young boy. "My father's a bastard and I don't want to be like him, so I don't want to do that to kids," he said. "I don't want to pass that gene onto the next generation."

As time went on, we'd have brief conversations about having children until he finally confided he actually could never have kids. I was stunned. Gabriel told me he went to a doctor while he was in his twenties and asked for a vasectomy. The doctor refused because of Gabriel's age stating, "You may regret it when you are a little older."

Determined not to be a father, Gabriel told me he brought someone else's kids to an appointment with a different doctor, and pretended they were his own: "I want to get snipped." This doctor agreed to the procedure. As much as I wanted to have children, I was devoted to Gabriel and loved him unconditionally. He'd been abused growing up and everybody left him. I reassured him, "We will always have each other and that will be enough." I had to let go of that dream. At least I had a lot of nieces and nephews to love and spoil.

I would come to realize that not having children with him was a blessing in disguise.

One day, I brought my two sweet godchildren for a visit to our house. I took them upstairs with me so they wouldn't be around to annoy him. We were having great fun, laughing together, when suddenly Gabriel appeared at my bedroom door.

"OK, the party's over," he announced, clapping his hands together.

"What do you mean the party's over? They just got here twenty minutes ago," I said, taken aback.

"It's time for them to go, Lisa," he said, as the kids looked on sheepishly.

I pushed back: "They're not bothering you. If you don't like it, you can go downstairs." Gabriel didn't say another word. He turned and left. I knew he was saving his reaction until we were alone. I took my niece and nephew home. They never visited our Dartmouth home again when Gabriel was around.

5

Groomed Victim

"Fawning is a people pleasing behaviour meant to avoid conflict in the short term, and fawning may prevent arguments and create a feeling of safety."[1]

COMMON CHARACTERISTICS
OF FAWNING BEHAVIOUR:

People-pleasing: doing things for others to gain their approval or to make others like you

Overly reliant on others: difficulty making decisions without other people's input

Prioritizing others' needs: ignoring your own needs, preferences, thoughts to please others

Being overly agreeable: having trouble saying no; your instinct is to appease the angry person

My sisters often called me a people pleaser—someone who often put the needs of others ahead of their own. They began to tell me I seemed to ignore my own needs as they watched my relationship with Gabriel develop. It would be almost two decades before a psychologist would explain the term *fawning* and how it took root in my long relationship.

After living together close to a year, Gabriel asked me to sign a paper forfeiting any claim to his assets. Offended, I told him it seemed unnecessary to me. I hadn't taken anything from my first husband when we got divorced, and I was not with Gabriel for his money, contrary to what others may have thought.

"Why would I sign something?" I asked. It shocked me that he would think I was money-hungry.

"Well, if you're not, then what is the issue?"

To me, it felt like he questioned my love for him.

I thought about what he said and signed it. I totally trusted him, with my money and my heart.

It didn't end up being anything official, as no lawyer was involved. I think he created the document himself, perhaps to test me. He didn't give me a copy of it, and he never brought it up again.

But there were other areas of my life he wanted to control.

Out of the blue, Gabriel told me it was time to get rid of my vehicle. "Sell that vehicle and we'll get you another one."

Initially, I resisted. "Mine is perfectly fine," I tried to tell him.

"I don't want you driving something you had with your ex-husband," he said.

His jealousy seemed like an overreaction; although when I thought about it, I understood that he didn't like the Jeep, as it was a reminder of my marriage. Gabriel promised that once I sold my Jeep, he would put the money toward getting me another vehicle. But as soon as it was gone, Gabriel waited months before getting me another vehicle. He said I could use his car if I needed to go anywhere. It started to make me feel uncomfortable because I had to "ask" to use it. I wasn't used to this, and when he wouldn't allow me to have it for whatever reason, I got mad. I felt like a kid begging a parent. I finally had enough; I wanted my own vehicle so I could go where I wanted, when I wanted. In the early years together, I felt more confident voicing my opinion. And he was *gentler* in disregarding it.

Gabriel finally found me a second-hand Alero. But it wasn't long before he expressed concern that I drove too often to see family and complained it put too much wear and tear on the car. Even though most of my closest family members lived within a twenty-kilometre radius of me, he suggested I visit them all in one day instead of spreading it throughout the week. I didn't like that, but understood the logic of monitoring mileage on my vehicle. Somehow, he had a way of convincing me his ideas were right, and if I questioned them, I was made to feel stupid. Besides, Gabriel got irritable when I stayed away from home too long, and I didn't want to have to deal with his moodiness. He could be happy one minute, then lecture me about something the next. I became good at making excuses for why I couldn't see my family as much. It just wasn't worth the tension I felt.

Gabriel tried but had no frame of reference to understand our Banfield clan and its complex dynamic. He rarely saw or spoke with his parents, so it baffled him that I called my sisters a couple of times a day. He often joked we were more like a cult, because we were so close.

"What are you talking to them about?" he'd badger me.

"Nothing, just everyday stuff," I would say and laugh it off. But I sensed he didn't like our strong connection because he wanted me all to himself. That's when he started to suggest that I should work for him.

When I first met Gabriel, I had just completed a hairdresser's course after working at the bank. I wanted to try something new, and I always liked styling hair and helping others look great. After a brief time working for a salon, I realized it wasn't as fulfilling as I'd hoped. When I expressed my disappointment about my job, he told me to quit.

"You don't need to work. I will take care of you," he assured me.

I thought about it, but I wanted to independently contribute to our life together. I liked to be busy and couldn't just sit around. I had worked since my teenage years, serving coffee at Tim Hortons. I liked interacting and socializing with people. As much as Gabriel wanted to take care of me, I needed to work.

I returned to banking as a teller, working just five minutes from our home. Often, he surprised me by popping into my work for a visit. Then he showered me with compliments. He was impressed by my professionalism and dedication to my clients.

"You really are a great worker, Lisa. You need to come work for me," he suggested again. "You wouldn't have to worry about trying to get time off; we could take vacations together and do whatever we wanted, when we wanted."

On the one hand, his faith in me boosted my self-esteem, and yet, I knew nothing about making dentures.

"I'll get you trained, and we can run the clinic together. It can be our business, and we can live the life we want," he said.

He made it sound like the ideal partnership. Anxious yet excited by the prospect of a new career, I agreed, though I had mixed feelings about working for Gabriel full time. I valued my sisters' opinions and I ran the idea by them. They had serious concerns. "I am a little nervous about that, just for your own independence," Maureen said, "but I can see the benefits of having a good trade and new skills."

In 2003, at thirty-five, I took a job at Schaefer Dental Lab to gain experience and confidence. I worked for a year there and quickly learned it was something I could adopt as my new career. Impressed by my work ethic and ability, my colleagues made me feel confident. I wanted to improve my skills. When Gabriel noticed how quickly I learned how to make dentures, he insisted I quit.

"Lisa, you are a natural at this," he praised me, genuinely surprised at my mastery of the trade. I knew he was proud of me. More importantly, I felt proud of myself and grew more confident as I contributed to the success of our business. "Let's work together as a team, just you and me."

The two of us were soon making a lot of money. We established a routine that worked for both of us. I'd wake early, prepare breakfast for him, and then prep the lab for the day's appointments. Gabriel would join me downstairs later that morning. We'd finish with morning clients, then he'd travel to the Halifax clinic while I continued to work on the dentures from our Dartmouth location. We'd have patients' dentures ready for pick-up the same day. That kind of turnaround was unheard of in this industry, as most clinics had to contract out the processing off-site, taking several weeks to complete. Word spread, and our patient roster grew exponentially.

As the business became more efficient and lucrative, Gabriel wanted us to look for a summer property he had always dreamed of owning. Driving throughout the countryside became our weekend pastime. Gabriel suggested the small town of Parrsboro, so we took the road along the Bay of Fundy. Although the area attracts tourists, the two-hour drive from our Dartmouth home seemed too far away to me. As we headed back toward the city, I noticed a sign that read *Cottage for Sale*. We drove down the dirt road to the rural beachside community of Portapique, 130 kilometres north of Dartmouth (just over an hour's drive). The beauty and simplicity of the rural area convinced us to make an offer on a log home that needed tender love and care. Despite the healthy cash flow of our business, Gabriel said he wanted to borrow the down payment from his parents and put their name on the land deed, a decision he would later regret. I now understand this was a means of hiding his true wealth.

Renovating the log cottage became our passion. For the more challenging work, Gabriel hired others to help him dig up the land, clear the lot, and raise the roof. Maureen's partner helped Gabriel build an engineered deck overlooking the spectacular Bay of Fundy. We spent all our weekends on the property. The physical work was exhausting but exhilarating at the same time. Every slate stone we placed by hand represented the sweat equity that helped accomplish our dream. The "cottage" transformed into a beautiful, winterized log home with plenty of windows that captured the picturesque view from sunset to sunrise.

By now, Gabriel took over all our finances. He had a knack for making money, and whenever I questioned why he did certain things—like dealing with so many different banks, having other companies, or storing cash in tins—he'd say for *tax reasons*. I never understood that part of the business but I trusted him as a successful businessman. I felt more secure in our future than ever before. My life seemed so big—though, in reality, my world was shrinking incrementally without my awareness.

PART II

Love Is Blind

When it was good, it was great.
When it was bad, it was brutal.

6

The First Assault

BEFORE WORKING FOR Gabriel, he needed help to run the two denture clinics. He hired another denturist he knew, Renée Baker, to help with the lab work. At that point I wasn't aware that Gabriel and she partied together previously. Looking back now, I'm certain I would have had an issue with him hiring her. He lied by omission.

When Renée invited us to a summer cottage party on Sutherland Lake, thirty minutes outside of Portapique, Gabriel felt he couldn't refuse the invitation, given their business relationship was so new. I was still quite shy and not much for crowds, especially with people I didn't know. I said to Gabriel, "The only way I will go is if you drive. I'm always the designated driver and I would like to have some drinks so I can relax and have a good time." He seemed fine with that. I wanted to make sure he wouldn't drink, so I reiterated, "Just so you know, I'm not spending the night there either."

"No problem; I'll drive."

Coincidentally, one of our Portapique neighbours was also hosting a low-key social around their firepit for community members that same weekend. It was such a beautiful day; we had a couple of drinks there before heading to Renée's. Gabriel stopped drinking so he could drive and soon told me we had to get going. I reluctantly agreed, hoping we could just make an appearance at the other party then return to this one where I felt more comfortable, and I could just walk home.

We took our Jeep and arrived at Sutherland Lake mid-afternoon with the outdoor party well underway. When we arrived Gabriel and I met up with Renée, who was very sweet and made me feel at ease. I made myself a drink and began to mingle with the other guests, who were in good spirits and friendly. The music played as people laughed and carried on in small groups around the property. By dusk, the drinks and conversation flowed as everyone seemed to be having a good time. It reminded me of our many family gatherings.

I spotted Gabriel with a beer in his hand. Social situations unnerved him. Alcohol helped him relax, and I could tell from the way he acted: This wasn't his first beer. Like a switch, my fun ended. As usual, I had to be the responsible one. When I approached him, he avoided my gaze. He knew he had broken his promise. He knew I was upset.

"Well, I'm done. You said you wouldn't drink," I complained.

"I only had a couple. We can just spend the night."

"I told you: I am not spending the night."

Clearly embarrassed to be arguing in front of others, he turned to Renée and sniped: "See what I have to put up with?"

I didn't hold back, "You don't have to put up with anything. If you want to stay, you stay. But I am going." I walked off to the Jeep.

He followed and jumped in the passenger side. I started driving as we argued back and forth.

"Why do you have to ruin everything?" he yelled.

"You told me you wouldn't drink, and you would drive us home."

"We could have just spent the night. Why do you have to be so stubborn? What's the big deal?"

"The big deal is I told you that I wanted to drink this time, and you said you would drive. Heaven forbid you let me have a good time for a change."

Without warning he struck my face with his hand. Stunned, I tried to process what happened. *Oh my God, did he just hit me?* I turned to look at him as though I had imagined it. He delivered another blow to my face. And another. I instinctively moved my hands to protect my face. I looked down and saw blood on my shirt. *I'm bleeding?* I was in shock and dazed by what he'd just done. My mind spun. I'd never been hit before.

My mind was in overdrive as I remembered a recent episode of *Oprah* about abduction and murder. *Never let them take you to a second location.* It was such a random thought, but at that moment, it came to me. *Don't leave with him. Run, don't let him catch you.* I stopped the Jeep and jumped out. I fled into the woods to get away from him.

I felt my heart pounding as I ran. I felt delirious as my pulse shot out of control. I was in full flight mode; I could hear him panting behind me. *Oh my God, what is happening? He's coming after me.* I felt the weight of my heart beating with a force that took my breath away. I saw a big tree and hid behind it, hoping he wouldn't see me. How naïve.

I jerked back to reality as his hand gripped my long hair and pulled me backward. I dropped. My scalp pierced with pain as my hair ripped free from the force of my fall. He pummeled my body in all directions. I winced, absorbing the force of his maddening punches as my arms sought protection for whatever part of me anticipated a hit. My brain, straining to comprehend the unreal: *Gabriel is beating me. The man I love is beating me.* It took a minute for my senses to register. Only then did I scream aloud for the first time. No distinct words, just sounds into the air. *Scream, keep screaming.*

Someone finally heard me.

I saw a glare of light illuminating Gabriel above me. He looked up, stopped, and ran. Dumbfounded, I was shaken to my core, but he was gone. I needed to find safety. I got up and kept moving in the opposite direction. If he came back, he would not find me.

My battered body ached, while my face stung. I heard a voice yelling, "Lisa, Lisa?" It was Renée. "Where are you? Come out?"

"No, I'm too scared. Can you come to me?"

In the dark, she followed my voice. She looked at me with such a reaction, it scared me. "Lisa, what happened?" she repeated frantically.

Weak and winded as the rush of adrenaline drained from me, I still couldn't believe what he'd done.

"Gabriel punched me. I don't even know what happened."

"Gabriel told me, you lost it. Oh my God, sweetie. It's going to be OK."

"I just want to go home."

Somehow Renée got me back to the road, where I saw a police car. I could see the figure in the back seat was Gabriel. This wasn't a dream. I had a sudden urge to vomit. Inconsolable and sore, I just had to get out of there. Renée took me to a nearby cottage where more strangers surrounded me, their faces aghast.

"I need to go home." I tried to get up.

A soft-spoken stranger held my arm down compassionately. "You can't drive like this. We'll take you home. You can't go there by yourself."

Another added, "Do you want to talk to the police?"

My heart spiked, "No." I became more and more agitated. "No, sorry, that will just make it worse. I just want to get my car and go home to Dartmouth. I don't want to get anybody involved." Distraught, I felt lucid instantly.

"OK. OK. Just stay here for a few hours until you are well enough to drive."

Though I appreciated they just wanted to help, their questions overwhelmed me. Embarrassed and scared, I just wanted to go home to my family.

I have no idea how long after, but they finally agreed I could drive. I couldn't wait to get out of there. Flashbacks distracted me from worrying about how I was going to find my way back. When I reached the end of the dirt road, I hit the asphalt and kept driving until I recognized an intersection that would take me to our cottage. I planned to go as far as the Portapique Cemetery next to our cottage, then walk to get my car so Gabriel wouldn't see or hear me.

I pulled over and turned off the Jeep. I noticed a neighbour stopped behind me. Then my driver's side door opened. Gabriel shouted, "Get out!"

"No problem," I mustered, still shaking but emboldened by anger at what he had done to me. He drove the Jeep to our cottage a few yards away.

I rushed to get inside our neighbour's truck. Ellison was a kind, elderly man. I knew I would be safe with him.

"What happened? What's going on?"

"Nothing, Ellison. I just want to get in my car and go home."

We approached the cottage where Gabriel paced on the front deck waiting for me. "Lisa, come in here. I won't hurt you," he coaxed.

"Are you crazy?"

I turned to Ellison, "I don't feel safe. Will you come in with me so I can get my keys and leave?"

Gabriel, steely-eyed, barked at Ellison, "This doesn't concern you. Go home. Lisa, come here; I won't hurt you."

I refused to move. Incensed, Gabriel got something from the open garage and went to my car. I began to shout. "Oh my God, he's taking the tires off my car! Do something! Ellison, can you please do something? I'm scared. I need my car to get home."

"I'm sorry, Lisa. I can't. It's not my property."

His response filled me with bold rage. How could another man stand by and watch this happen and not do anything? "Are you a coward or a man?" I yelled at him.

Even he feared Gabriel. I was terrified to get out of the truck by myself and give Gabriel another chance to hurt me. Exasperated, I scoffed at Ellison, "Just take me back then and I will call someone to come get me." There was no way I was going near Gabriel.

Ellison took me to the nearby house where people were still partying from earlier that day, so I could use their phone. When they looked at me and my bloody white shirt, they asked me what happened. In a sick, twisted way, I tried to protect Gabriel. I didn't want the neighbours to think badly of him. I told them I didn't want to talk about it. Feelings of shame and disbelief filled me. I didn't want my sisters to know either, so I called my niece, Stephanie. I knew she would come get me and take me back to our home in Dartmouth.

After driving for ninety minutes, Stephanie arrived. Pregnant and tired, she had just driven through heavy drizzle. The rural roads were darker than usual; she was justly upset. She didn't look at me as I got in her car. "What's going on? Are you two fighting again?" she asked me.

"It wasn't a good scene. It got really bad."

"What do you mean, bad?"

I couldn't bring myself to tell her. Bruised and cut from his punches, I couldn't even cry. I was exhausted and bewildered. The dried blood on my ripped clothes darkened into a deep, dirty red colour.

Then the lamppost light shone in the car, and she shrieked when she saw me, "Oh my God, what happened to you? You're bleeding! What happened?!" She pulled to the shoulder of the road. "Your face is swollen; what did he do?" She was more hysterical than me.

"Gabriel went ballistic. We got into an argument, and he just punched me and kept hitting me."

"I'm taking you to the police in Truro."

"No, I just want to go home."

"You need to report this!" she insisted.

"No, Stephanie. I can't. It won't be happening again. I'm done."

"Let me take you to the hospital then."

"No, just take me home, please."

Stephanie knew how stubborn I could be and didn't want to agitate me further. "You're coming to my house then."

"Just promise me you won't tell anyone." She agreed.

I shrank into my quiet place as I replayed the entire ghastly evening. We drove in silence until we arrived at her home. She helped me upstairs then ran me a warm bath. She sat on the tub's edge with me while gently washing off my bloody body. My spirit was broken.

In the morning, I awakened to Maureen's warm hug and sorrowful face. Stephanie had called her to help. They tried once again to get me to go to the police or the hospital, but I refused. "We need to eat least take pictures, in case you change your mind," Maureen insisted.

"Fine," I said, "but promise me you won't show them to anyone."

I grimaced with embarrassment as she took pictures of my face, neck, and upper torso. I just wanted the nightmare over. Maureen took me to her house. I felt so desperate. What was I going to do? Both she and Stephanie tried to make me feel better about myself and my future but my body didn't believe them. They were visible bruises of shame.

Before doing anything else, I needed my car. I got a ride to Portapique the next day. I knew Gabriel's parents were scheduled to visit from New Brunswick, so I could get my car without incident. Gabriel didn't like people knowing his business. He always wanted things to appear perfect.

Just as I suspected, my car was parked in the driveway, all four tires on, as if nothing had happened. His mom and dad were doing yard work. I'm not sure what Gabriel said to them about my absence, but when I walked up the driveway, his mom took one look at me and frantically asked, "Are you OK?"

"Do I look OK?" I asked, pointing to my swollen and bruised face. "This is what your son did to me." I was done filtering.

We didn't have a great relationship. I couldn't trust her. She'd be nice to my face but then talk about me to Gabriel behind my back. I refused to pretend anymore.

I didn't even wait for her response. Gabriel came out from the garage as I walked to the front door. "I'm here for my keys and to get some of my things." I tried to ignore him. I just opened the door and headed to my bedroom. Gabriel followed me, trying to defend his actions.

"It's your fault. If you just would have stayed, this wouldn't have happened. You ruined a good time. It's all your fault."

"Yeah," sarcastically pointing to my face, "this is my fault." I gathered a few items from my closet as he continued to berate me. His mom came around the corner, but I avoided getting into it with her. I got my keys and left.

I moved in with Maureen in Dartmouth until I figured out what to do. I felt lost and alone. Once the shock had worn off and my bruises had healed, I wondered how Gabriel was doing without me. I hated that I missed him. Of course, I thought only of the sweet and loving memories we shared. Perhaps he had already moved on with someone else? Perhaps he was done with me? Maybe I made a mistake? Maybe this was just a bad night? I know he didn't mean to do it; he was drinking. We all make mistakes. All I could think about was that little lost boy and his suffering. It made me question if I had overreacted. The truth is that I felt sorry for him, and I still loved him.

My sisters encouraged me to move on, to forget about Gabriel. They thought I moved too fast and fell too hard for him. I didn't tell them that he called me and left messages: "I miss you, and can you please answer." It was difficult not to respond, but it felt good that he was reaching out.

One evening, several weeks later, I heard a tap on my bedroom window. I knew it was Gabriel. He looked so sad and pleaded for me to come outside to talk. I thought I owed him that, at least. I snuck out of Maureen's basement without her knowing. Once I saw his face etched with pain, I listened to him, hearing everything I needed to hear to open my heart—yet again.

"I was drinking. It was my fault. I got out of control," he told me. "I am so sorry. Lisa, I promise you. It will never happen again. I love you." And on and on. I knew I would give him a second chance. My cycle of domestic abuse had begun.

7

Living the Lie

DURING THE FIRST five years together, I became a shadow of myself: discounting my beliefs, my morals, and my own thoughts. I quieted those. They never died within me; they were hibernating so that I might survive in the inhabitable cold that became my life.

Looking back, I see how Gabriel controlled me. He commented on what I wore, my hair, what I ate, where I went, what I drove, who I saw. But his grip happened so gradually, I didn't recognize the hold he had over me. I'm embarrassed to share the time Gabriel told me to get a nose job to get rid of a small bump. He had a way of making me feel insecure about my looks.

"I'm fine with my nose," I told him.

He'd ignore my words as if my feelings about my own body didn't matter. He went ahead and booked an appointment for a rhinoplasty. My old insecurities rose up and my fawning default to please him prevailed. When I got to the office, the surgeon looked at me and said, "There's nothing wrong with your nose."

I agreed but I pushed my thoughts aside and pandered to Gabriel's wishes. I decided to go through with the operation. Another regret.

***

By now, we were consumed with work. I made the sets of dentures, while Gabriel determined the clients' denture needs. My long day extended into the night as the processing demands increased. I also worked weekends to ensure the patients' dentures would be ready for Monday morning pick-up. I had some free time because Gabriel regularly travelled to Portapique after a late Wednesday shift, but outside of clinic hours, I remained on call 24/7. Gabriel never used or owned a cellphone. I can't imagine that, but he told me: "I talk to people all day and I don't want to be bothered on my own time. Besides, people don't need to know where I am all the time. You can email or call the neighbours if you need me when I'm at the cottage."

I understood his point, but that meant that all of the business calls were forwarded to my private cell. My sisters shared their concerns that it wasn't right. But of course, Gabriel didn't care.

"You don't even have a life. He gets to take off and you're left to do all the work," Janice said to me one day.

It bothered Janice and Maureen, but I liked that Gabriel was so proud of me. He got excited to see unprecedented productivity with the company. He valued my work ethic and ability. He'd often say, "Let's work really hard the next few years, make a lot of money, then retire and do whatever we want."

Gabriel's business mind churned constantly—anything to make a buck. He found clients on government assistance who needed false teeth. He would visit hospitals, and we'd service patients there so they didn't have to be transported. Soon word got out about his "home visits." He'd also waive the co-pay portion for people on social assistance to grow his client base. Our regular clients paid up to $3,000 for a pair of dentures. With my efficient on-site processing, a pair of dentures cost less than $500 to make. Our profit margin skyrocketed.

We both benefited from his business formula and the revenue that came with it. Gabriel was a master at working the system to benefit himself financially. He alone managed the books, and often had me request cash from clients whenever possible. Any cash I collected during the day, he told me to store in a safe that was hidden in the wall of our clinic. Some days I'd collect thousands of dollars. If anyone tried to pay by credit card, that made him angry, so I always asked for cash. I did as he asked, and he trusted me. When our clinic's portable safe reached a certain amount, he told me to bring it up to the cottage in Portapique. I didn't dare question his business practices.

Eager to impress other people about his success, Gabriel rarely credited me for my role. He would always make me feel like I could do no wrong, and the next minute tear me down like I'm dirt under his feet. Janice recognized my contribution to the business and always stood up for me when Gabriel would brag about his success in front of her. He and Janice often sparred like brother and sister.

"You know what, Gabe? You may have started the Atlantic Denture Clinic, but it's Lisa who is doing all the work. You wouldn't have this kind of success without her, and you know it," she pointed out to him.

Janice's directness could infuriate Gabriel. My stomach would be in knots when the two of them bantered. I dreaded their confrontations; I didn't want him upset, as it could come back on me later. Janice had no idea I'd pay the price after she left. I became very good at pretending everything was OK, even to my sisters. It drove Janice wild when he'd brag about his material wealth, like the cars and motorbikes he owned.

"Janice, you need to find someone like me," he teased her with a big wide grin.

"Yeah, OK, Gabe. You're the man," she mocked sarcastically.

Even with our success, Gabriel still managed to qualify for the GST rebate cheques; he was always reading and researching loopholes when it came to the government. I never challenged or questioned the way it all worked. I had no idea of the intricacies of business. All I knew was that we were successful, and our future was secure.

Our lifestyle looked nothing like the humble beginnings I'd known growing up in our tiny Beaver Bank home. I admit I got used to a certain lifestyle. While he collected tools, cars, and land, I bought clothing, shoes, jewellery, and gifts for my family and friends. I'd buy so many outfits that the price tags would still be on them months later. The freedom I felt while I shopped was addictive. I defaulted to my past need for control over my life and became a shopaholic. But for me shopping had nothing to do with materialism. I had lost so much control of my life by then, that this gave me power over something.

Being together day and night began to take its toll. His moods became increasingly extreme. My hypervigilance escalated as I waited for the next thing that would set him off. He could morph from Dr. Jekyll to Mister Hyde in a split second, especially when he drank. Living with him day to day was like a roller coaster, a wooden one that creaked and moaned until it lost control and went off the rails. There would be no reason for it: He'd just lose it, and I would try to calm him down. A cycle I would come to know well.

If I made a mistake or something happened to a denture during processing, he would holler at me, often in front of patients. Not only was I humiliated, but it made it all the harder to fix, as I was under further pressure to perform while being made to feel totally inept. I thought about quitting our business at one point, but didn't know where I could go. Back to the bank? Try another clinic? When I dared to suggest that to Gabriel, he mocked me. His praise had long disappeared.

"Nobody is going to hire you," he'd say, making me feel inadequate. I lacked the confidence to try. In the end I just accepted this was part of my life with him.

Compartmentalizing helped me cope. I had to focus on the good stuff or I wouldn't be able to live with the reality of my life as he became more controlling, and physically abusive. Sometimes Gabriel's actions didn't make sense. If I was sick, he would get me the medicine I needed and do whatever he could to help me feel better. But he would also hurt me deeply.

I didn't understand how somebody could be so cruel and wounding one minute, then sweet and compassionate the next. I lived each day trying my best not to tick him off. I could never predict what would come next.

* * *

Gabriel liked to travel. "Let's go to the Dominican Republic," he decided one day. I had never been to an all-inclusive resort, so it was exciting to do something different. With the intensity of my work schedule, the idea of glorious tropical weather and relaxing by the beach sounded like a perfect escape.

Once at the resort, we got into an argument about something. I went to the buffet alone because Gabriel didn't feel like going. On this night, when I got back to our room, he was gone; no note and no way to contact him. I stewed for hours in the room waiting for him to return, fretting that he was off somewhere doing God knows what. I was so angry but also worried. We were in a different country and I had no idea where he'd gone. I was just about ready to contact resort security when the suite phone rang. I rushed to answer it.

"Brinnnggggg," he jokingly made the ring sound. "Would you like to come out for supper now?" he said in a fake British accent. He would always make light of a situation like this. It was his way of apologizing.

"What do you want?" I asked, annoyed at first.

But by the end of the conversation, he had me laughing and my anger melted away. I didn't like the way he acted sometimes, but I always forgave him and blamed myself for bringing on one of his moods—or worse. It must have been something I said or did, I would reason with myself.

Until later that trip:

JOURNAL ENTRY: APRIL 2005:

Well, today is Thursday and yesterday Gabriel was awful to me. He really scared me. It's like I can't do anything right around him. He grabbed me by the neck, smashed me in the head and tore my shorts practically off me and ripped my good bathing suit off me. He said that he would take great pleasure in taking my head and smashing it through the wall. I started to scream, which made him more angry. He made me sit in a chair, while he lazed in bed, calling me a stupid bitch, loser, that I'm an idiot with no intelligence.

Perhaps the only people who knew the dark side of Gabriel were his parents.

Feeling generous, Gabriel paid for his parents to vacation with us in Cuba in 2016. During the first few days, things went smoothly as we adventured on the catamaran and even tried parasailing. Gabriel, a risk-taker at heart, went first. They harnessed us up on the beach. I couldn't stop shaking as I waited for my turn. His dad went up second, and you could tell he was having a ball. When my turn came, I freaked out. As I rose into the sky, gripping onto the straps, all I kept thinking was, *I will never do this again*. I am not a thrill-seeker. I can't believe I even tried it. But I feared disappointing Gabriel or provoking him.

Midway through our family trip, liquor got the better of Gabriel as we hung by the poolside in the scorching sun. Gabriel and his father had been drinking all day and started talking about the past. As dinner time neared, his mother and I returned to the hotel to get dressed. We tried to coax them to join us at the restaurant, but Gabriel and his father wanted to stay at the pool and drink.

Just as we sat down, people we had met earlier came into the restaurant telling us: "Your husband and father-in-law are fighting."

We ran out and saw Gabriel smashing his father's head on the concrete by the pool. Blood gushed everywhere. "Apologize for abusing me! I was just a child," he insisted.

His dad refused and, worse, kept denying he ever did anything to Gabriel.

"Just say you're sorry," Gabriel's mother pleaded with her husband. He wouldn't, and the blood kept running.

Resort security hurried over as people started to gather and watch Gabriel lose all control. The staff wanted to call the police, but his father yelled at them: "No, leave him."

Gabriel left the pool area. I ran to our room where Gabriel appeared in the door—smiling. "I finally beat him," he bragged. I felt disgusted by the whole scene. What kind of person hurts his own father?

Not getting the response he wanted from me, he went into the bathroom.

Within minutes, his father knocked on our door, his face swollen beyond recognition. He asked to talk to me alone. Oh God, I thought, *What now?* I followed him to his room, wondering what he would say.

When I sat down on the bed, I felt bad for how horrible his face looked. He was clearly in a lot of pain.

"I was a bastard to my wife; I was a bastard to my son and Gabriel's going to do the same thing to you. You need to leave him," he warned me.

I stood there awkwardly, wiping the draining tears from my eyes, as he admitted to me what Gabriel wanted to hear for himself. "Don't tell him I said this," said his father. "He'll do more damage to me and come after me again."

When I returned to our room, I didn't dare tell Gabriel what his dad said. After his rage, he'd escape then return calm as if nothing happened. His parents avoided any contact with us for the remainder of the week.

I understood why he tried to get his father to own up to his actions, but he went about it the wrong way. He didn't feel safe or loved by his parents, who weren't nurturing people. From the time I met Gabriel, he called them by their first names only, never Mom or Dad. I wanted him to experience love and care. I wanted him to know that I would always be there for him despite his mistakes. I'd heard enough stories from Gabriel that gave me deep empathy for him. One that still haunts me was his father taking his baby blanket and burning it in front of him saying, "You're too old for this; you don't need it."

I came to realize that, as much as Gabriel hated how his father treated people, he became just like him. The first assault at Sutherland Lake was not an isolated incident. I couldn't bear to tell my sisters of the pain that had become my life. There were so many abusive moments I couldn't share with anyone. When they'd ask if he did it again, I would just say no.

Over the course of our relationship, we developed an unhealthy jealousy. His flirting with others created paranoia for both of us. He liked having me as eye candy, but when men noticed me, he got really incensed. During one of our Florida trips, we went to a high-end shopping centre that carried all the top designers. I wore a white Calvin Klein fitted dress and carried a Michael Kors purse. At that moment, I felt like I belonged in the world. I walked differently, confidently. Then he told me to walk ahead of him so he could watch how people reacted to me. He seemed fascinated with human nature and, as bizarre as it sounds, I did as he asked. Strangers smiled and a couple of women came up to me and said how great I looked: "Where did you get that dress? You look so chic."

He relished in testing me. When other men showed me attention, he assumed I would cheat on him. While I would never betray him, I suspected he was cheating on me, as he did on his ex-wife years ago. He had a lot of time on his own, especially when he'd leave for the cottage midway through the week. When I joined him one weekend, I felt things were out of place from where I had left them. He told me he slept in my room and must have moved things. I didn't believe him. As a test, I placed something in my room a certain way to see if it changed. It didn't matter; he always had an excuse, and, in the end, I had no proof. I should have trusted my intuition.

Then one night, the phone rang at 1 a.m. Normally I would let it go to the answering machine, as patients called at all hours of the night. For some reason, I picked it up. It was a woman who claimed to be a nurse for Gabriel's Uncle Glynn. I thought, *Oh God, did something happen to him?* I woke up Gabriel and passed him the phone.

"Don't ever call here again," he said and hung up.

"What's going on? Who's that?" I asked him.

"It's nothing, Lisa. Just go to bed," he said.

I knew he was lying, but, as usual, not to anger him further, I let it go.

Another time, we'd been enjoying a warm summer night in the backyard of our Dartmouth home. I listened to him talk about all he'd done with the clinic and the property as we sipped our drinks. I had gone inside and changed into something sexy, then I opened the window: "The party's inside; come on in," I flirted enticingly.

"I'll be in shortly," he said as he finished his beer.

I closed the window. I gazed out a few times and there he remained in solitude. Eventually I gave up waiting, got undressed, and fell asleep. I woke up in the middle of the night and saw he wasn't in the bedroom. *Where the hell is he?*

I went outside and drove to the end of the street to see if he was in the bars. When I didn't see him, I returned home where I sat in the truck and waited for him to come home. My anxiety and anger rose.

I looked next door at a two-storey crack house, where a lot of girls were coming and going. I thought I saw a tall guy through the veiled curtains but wasn't sure. I got tired of waiting for him, so I went to bed. I had to work the next day and needed sleep.

Gabriel came through the door around 7 a.m. I asked him where he was, expecting him to come clean. "Trust me," he said. "If there's any time, I need you to listen to me, it is now. Just go to work and we will talk when you get home."

Although I went to work, I left early. My stomach in knots, I kept thinking, *What the hell is going on?* I needed to know what happened. When Gabriel left for Halifax, I asked Renée. He shared a lot with Renée, who shared a lot with me.

I knew it. Just as I suspected, he told her he spent the night next door. It was known to be a hangout for people using drugs. Gabriel put up a high fence to protect our property from the transients who lived there.

I was furious. I left the clinic and banged on their door. There was no answer, but I could see people were home. I kept banging.

Two women finally opened the door.

I was curt. "Was Gabriel here last night?"

"Yes, he was here all night," said one of the girls.

"Just tell me the truth. I deserve to know the truth," I asked them point-blank, "Did you sleep together?"

They called him a pig, and one admitted she slept with him.

I finally had the proof I needed. When Gabriel came home, I came out of the house and confronted him. "You make me sick. I know where you were."

At that very moment, one of the girls he'd been with last night walked up the driveway to speak with him.

"Get the hell off my property," he ordered. She was startled by his reaction and turned back immediately.

I stormed off to the house as he kept telling me that it meant nothing. He loved me and that was just sex. He told me not to worry about them, as if that would make it OK. He said he was sorry, and it wouldn't happen again. I started grabbing a few of my belongings. I had to get out of there; I'd had enough.

"Get away from me; you make me sick." I left.

I went to Maureen's. Soon after, I moved into her basement.

Several weeks later, Gabriel knocked at my window begging me to come back.

"I was drinking. I'm sorry. Lisa, I swear to you it won't happen again."

For a while it was fine; he did enough to give me false hope that everything would be OK and that he had changed. Ever the optimist, I began each day telling myself what I'm grateful for and I'd write them down in my journal. I got much-needed relief when Gabriel would go to the cottage by himself. I'd stay home and visit with family and friends.

Bingo with my sisters on Sunday became my favourite thing to do. We would laugh and be silly. I could be myself, carefree, and not worry about what Gabriel needed or wanted. It worked out well until his jealousy crept in. He became paranoid, thinking someone would flirt with me at the bingo hall. He told me not to go because it was Sunday night, and he'd be coming back from the cottage and wanted us to hang out together.

I stayed home and waited as I watched the clock turn 8 p.m. Where was Gabriel? By now I realized he'd only said that so that I would not go out. He wanted me home even if he wasn't there. I was pissed when he walked through the door at 10 p.m. He told me he had a few drinks in him, which was always a warning that things could get ugly.

"What took you so long? I waited for you. I could have gone to bingo."

"Where do you think I was?" he baited me.

I could see this wasn't going to end well. "I'm tired; I'm going to bed," I said and turned away.

He lost it on me. He didn't like it when I walked away from him. He stormed into my bedroom and grabbed my neck.

"You little bitch," he yelled.

"Gabriel, stop—I can't breathe," I pleaded.

"I don't care," he spewed loudly in my face. He gave my throat one last squeeze, then left me gasping for air.

In the morning, we had to work together in the clinic downstairs. I didn't want it to be awkward all day, so I made him breakfast and delivered it to him in bed.

"I'm still mad at you," I said quietly. That was all I needed to let it go.

I was getting better at finding ways around his overt control of me. From then on, I went to bingo without telling him and was home in bed before he got back from Portapique.

***

Gabriel knew how much I valued being with my siblings, nieces, and nephews and to celebrate birthdays and Christmas. He said he never liked the family thing, so after years of trying, he suggested that I spend the holidays with my family; he'd go up to the cottage and wait for me.

"That way, we'll have our own Christmas time, just the two of us," he offered.

I'm sure others thought it was weird, or that I was a bad person for not spending Christmas with my partner, but it worked for us. Since he suggested it, that was our tradition. It was so much better than having to explain to my family why Gabriel wasn't there. Besides, they preferred not to socialize with him.

Mom never liked Gabriel. She couldn't "take to him." She said he didn't look her in the eyes, and she found him sneaky. By age seventy, Mom had moved into a nursing home. Since her brain aneurysm, her dementia got worse, and Dad couldn't look after her. The women in the family found a nursing home in Beaver Bank, so it was close to our home on Quarry Road. Each of us took turns visiting her every day she lived there. Often, we'd pick her up so she could spend the day with Dad. I'd also take her out for a ride or play cards with her. Mom missed having fast food, so that would always be a part of our visit.

When we learned she was dying of lung cancer, we spent more time ensuring she was never alone. On Mom's final day, May 16, 2008, everyone left for the night. Janice and I remained. We cried, nestled on either side of her, and kissed her goodbye as she took her last rattled breath.

Mom's funeral was like Old-Home Week. Our childhood church was overfilled with family and friends who adored Beulah. On behalf of our family, Maureen paid tribute with an endearing and funny eulogy. The tears and laughter filled every pew and rafter. We played "Green, Green Grass of Home" by Tom Jones, one of her favourites.

Gabriel sat next to me. Though I appreciated that he came, I felt little comfort from his presence. I wanted to sit among my brothers and sisters, whose love I craved in that moment.

It wasn't until the reception in the church hall that I noticed David, my first love, in the crowd. I hadn't seen him for years and feared Gabriel wouldn't be pleased my ex-boyfriend was here. My mind raced. I couldn't even mourn properly, as I couldn't predict Gabriel's reaction. He never met David, but Gabriel's jealousy could turn vicious without warning.

I had to get David out of there, so I walked toward him. We embraced briefly as I was skittishly aware of Gabriel's death stare from the corner of the room. David really liked Mom, and it was mutual. I wish I had more time, but I told David that Gabriel was here, and I didn't want anything to happen. David felt my discomfort and sympathetically left before anything could happen.

Who had I become?

Secrecy enveloped my day-to-day life. Like many women in abusive relationships, I was in total denial of my reality. Survival meant focusing on the here-and-now. I learned to compartmentalize my fear of Gabriel and to smile as though my life behind closed doors didn't exist. My optimism that things would get better blurred life's truth. They say love is blind. Although there were periods when Gabriel wasn't physically violent, his emotional abuse and coercive control worsened each year.

Our fighting became a pattern: "I've always been there for you," I'd say.

He'd ask me all the time, "You're such a good person, why do you love me?" It didn't matter how I responded; he never believed he was lovable.

I'd tell him, "You deserve to be loved, especially after the childhood you had."

He once told me his father put a gun in his hand and said, "I know you want to kill me, so kill me." Gabriel admitted that he almost did.

He also told me that his mother enabled the situation by telling his father whenever Gabriel acted up. "She knew he'd beat me, but she told him anyway." That made me so sad. He called his parents "repeat offenders" because they never changed.

His oldest friend, Tom Evans, was the only person Gabriel seemed to trust. Gabriel respected the successful New Brunswick lawyer. Tom got his pilot licence and owned properties. Gabriel always told me that he viewed Tom as his confidant. Gabriel admired his intelligence and wit. Tom must have felt the same way, because when he died in November 2009, he left everything to Gabriel: his properties, guns, and money. Tom's siblings tried to sue Gabriel over the estate but lost in court. For years, Gabriel really missed him. I don't think he ever got over his death.

Prior to his death, Tom witnessed Gabriel abuse me. He and a few friends were helping Gabriel work on the cottage renovations. They were all outside this summer day when Gabriel came into my bedroom. He had a few drinks that led to a fight about something that escalated. Suddenly, he jumped on top of me and started choking me. I screamed at him to stop.

Tom heard me from outside, "Gabriel, leave her alone. Come out with us."

As soon as Gabriel left me, I escaped through my bedroom's patio door to our neighbours, Brenda and George Forbes. They had retired from the military and moved to Portapique in 2002. We socialized a bit and they came to our cottage for drinks occasionally. Brenda invited me for an afternoon garden party, but Gabriel would make me come home because he didn't like me having too good a time. More than once, she'd see him grab my arm and end our visit abruptly.

On this day, Brenda could see my heightened distress. "We need to call the police," she urged.

But I pleaded with her not to: "It would only make it worse." Wanting help, yet too afraid to get anyone involved, the thought of what could happen terrified me into silence—and, in turn, silenced others. I felt confused and trapped. "I've gotta go back. I don't know what he'll do if he finds out I left." By this time, I was hyperventilating.

When I headed back toward the cottage, Tom and the other guys were sitting in front of the garage. As soon as Gabriel saw me, he bolted toward me and started chasing me around the cars. The guys just sat there and watched as if it were a game. I was embarrassed and humiliated. He got hold of me and took me into the house. "Don't you ever leave like that again."

I stayed inside the whole day. When supper time came, Gabriel stormed into my bedroom, "Make them something to eat."

I reluctantly obeyed him to avoid another beating. The guys sat waiting at the dining table for their supper while Gabriel went to his bedroom. He didn't even eat. I fed them quietly and none of them asked if I was okay or defended me for what they had seen. Without even a thanks from the men, I returned to my bedroom for the night.

I ran to Bo's for help another time. Gabriel was in a rage about something and had blocked my car in the driveway so I couldn't leave. Brenda tried once again to get me to call the police, a shelter, or other support. "You need to get help and there's a lot of help out there," she encouraged me.

But I couldn't. I was just too afraid to involve any authorities. "I don't want him going after my family," I confided in her.

Once again, I walked back to the cottage, hoping Gabriel had cooled down. He stood there and forbade me from ever going to Bo's again. I learned later through the public inquiry that Brenda reported Gabriel to the RCMP. No one followed up with her, so nothing came of her reporting the assault. But Gabriel had it in for her after that, and would taunt her to such an extreme that she feared for her life as well. The Forbes eventually sold their place in Portapique and moved away.

By now, we had fallen into a pattern that I now realize is typical of women in abusive relationships. I would try to calm him down when he got violent. I would threaten to leave for good, but then I would go back with him again and again. I wanted to leave so many times, but Gabriel knew how to keep me there by threatening to come after my family.

"I know where your family lives," he would warn. I couldn't take the chance he was bluffing. And so I fell into a deep hole, an abyss I couldn't escape. I felt alone and paralyzed to do anything.

My journals revealed the ugly truth; I was living with a monster:

JOURNAL ENTRY: NOV. 19, 2005:

Well this weekend wasn't the greatest, especially tonight. Gabriel and I got into it about Renée and he was very abusive, mentally and physically. He not only degraded me but threatened to kill me. Tonight I was really scared for my life! He was drinking yet again and by the way he was talking, I really thought he had nothing to lose. He said he would beat me silly then blow my head off, then kill himself if I left him. I was in the midst of getting ready to leave when he said this. He told me to get undressed then treated me like dirt, calling me a stupid cunt, and no wonder he gives me a beating from time to time.

Unbeknownst to me when I was away from the house, he found my journals and started reading them. When I came back, he'd confront me: "Why would you write that about me in your journal?"

"You have no right to read my journals. These are my personal thoughts," I said, clutching the notebook against my chest. Gabriel grabbed it from my hands. His fury stunned me given he was in the wrong. He stomped to the bathroom and threw it in the toilet. I got up and fished it out of the bowl. The ink, blurred, was dripping off the soaked pages. I had to throw them in the garbage. I felt so violated. I couldn't even have my own thoughts. And now my journals were another thing I had to hide. He yelled in my face so loud I couldn't take it anymore.

"I'm leaving," I said and rushed down to my car, finally trying to break free.

Gabriel raced after me. I managed to get to the garage and into my car. I released the garage door using my remote, but Gabriel stopped it manually and disconnected the unit from the wall. His imposing body stood in front of my hood so I couldn't move. He picked up a baseball bat and threatened to smash my windshield. When I didn't move, he pulled me out of the car: "You're not leaving. Get in the house," he ordered. "I know where they live, Lisa," he said, again.

"What's that supposed to mean?"

"You know what it means."

8

Sisters' Dilemma

MY CLOSEST SISTERS visited me in Portapique, where we hung out together despite their apprehension about Gabriel. Their attempts to get me to leave him never worked. I covered up so much since the first assault because I didn't want them to stop visiting me.

MAUREEN:

It is painful to witness your loved one losing her voice. As years passed, Lisa filtered her entire life through Gabriel. Every single decision she would make needed to pass the test of, *How will Gabriel react?* We watched her skittishness turn to distress, impacting her daily life and sadly, her soul. Eventually, Lisa became a shell of herself. Our Lisa became Gabriel's puppet, and the strings he controlled became unbreakable chains. Despite our efforts to get her to leave him, we grew discouraged and helpless; we realized she would stay with him forever. Sometimes, I witnessed his physical markings even though Lisa would lie about how her injuries happened. He was savvy enough never to hit her in the family's presence. However, his extreme dominance scared me.

Lisa would always move in with me following a serious episode. But once I had my little girl, Emma, I could no longer risk having her stay in my home. With fewer options, I found Lisa withholding more about what was really happening in their relationship. While I knew they still fought, I had no idea he was insidiously assaulting her. I was busy raising my girl and working for the Halifax Regional School Board. I was stunned to learn all the details of her persistently abusive life in the aftermath of 2020.

Since Emma would be with her dad alternate weekends, my long-time partner and I became frequent weekend house guests in Portapique. While the men worked on the myriad projects Gabriel had on the go, us girls had time to catch up. I looked forward to going up as I got to spend extended time with Lisa.

Though my partner and Gabriel were uniquely different they both were intellectuals and hard workers. They spent hours working together fixing or creating things: electrical, plumbing, mechanics, and construction. They were fascinated by the intricacies of design and revelled in the labour of constructing such a huge building from scratch. When the time came to build a garage on a property near the cottage, Gabriel wanted to add a loft to the upstairs apartment for overnight guests. The "warehouse," as they named it, would become a gathering center, the place for entertainment where people would gather and socialize. From the clearing of the land to framing and finishing work, they played like schoolboys throughout the day and admired the efforts of their work over beer and conversation at night.

To the extent Gabriel was capable of connection, they bonded.

We'd have huge bonfires, listen to tunes, laugh, and talk about having future adventures together. Alcohol helped to diffuse Gabriel's eccentricities, like his obsession with collecting things, everything from toilet paper to motorcycles. He boasted about his expensive items and how he managed to get a super deal because he was so smart.

We couldn't understand Gabriel's constant need for praise. We tolerated that part of him. Though my partner didn't share all the details of their conversations, he shared with me: "Gabriel's not quite right." He felt uncomfortable with Gabriel's scheming about how he could make more money and how he said a lot of inappropriate things.

One of the scariest foretelling of Gabriel's sickness occurred on June 2, 2010, nine years into their relationship.

The incident was spurred on by the loan Gabriel received from his father years earlier to pay for the cottage. Though Gabriel had enough money to buy it outright, he hid his true wealth to avoid taxes. Though his parents loaned him the money, they insisted on holding the deed jointly until it was paid off. Trouble erupted when Gabriel returned all their money plus interest, and yet his parents refused to remove their names from the deed. Lisa shared the dramatic updates with me as they unfolded.

Gabriel and his parents always had a tumultuous relationship, based on control. Gabriel was always told he was a mistake, so when his mother got pregnant again, his parents gave up the second child for adoption. They didn't tell Gabriel until he was forty years old, after the Wortmans were contacted by their second son wanting to meet his birth parents. Gabriel could hardly believe he had a brother. It sent him into a spin. They wanted Gabriel to join in the reunion. And as when Gabriel was a child, they had the upper hand. They leveraged releasing the cottage deed if Gabriel came to the reunion. Gabriel never tolerated threats from others. Things had become intolerable, and Gabriel became unhinged.

I didn't know how dire the situation was until Lisa called me: "Maureen, I need you. Gabriel left. He's going to kill his parents," she blurted out.

"What?! What are you talking about?"

"I don't know what to do. He just went crazy. He's lost his mind. He took his gun. I don't know what to do," Lisa said.

"Did you call the police?"

"No! They will kill him. He's got a gun."

"Jesus, Lisa. Stay there. I'm coming over."

By the time I arrived at Lisa's, Gabriel had returned. His eyes looked vacant; his posture slumped as he sat on the stool in the small dining room off the kitchen. He seemed listless and lethargic. His voice was low and matter-of-fact, saying, "I'm done. I don't care what happens to me. I hate them."

We tried to shake him out of his stupor. "Gabriel, no. You can't be serious." But his words became more and more disturbing: "No one will recognize them. I will chop them up and smear their blood on the walls, then I'll kill myself."

Horrified, I never heard anything so evil. "Gabriel, you need help," I tried to tell him, as my throat became instantly dry. I eyed Lisa as if to say, *We are out of our depths here. This man is psychotic.*

"I need a beer," Gabriel said flatly.

Lisa jumped up and I followed her into the kitchen. Lisa then showed me the hole in the wall where Gabriel fired his gun earlier that night. "Oh my God, Lisa. This is serious. He is sick! He needs help. We need to call the police."

"No, Gabriel will lose it. He won't back down, Maureen. They will kill him. Gabriel's uncle is a retired RCMP officer. He knows what's happening and has already warned his parents. Gabriel's home now. It's over. It will be OK." It was like Lisa engaged some kind of Stepford autopilot, a hopeful pretence I quickly adopted, as the reality of what was happening was too frightening to process.

Lisa got him a beer, and we returned to the dining room. I tried to offer suggestions for therapy. Gabriel calmly continued to drink and listen but I could tell nothing was registering. I don't remember how long I stayed or what else was said. I couldn't believe this was real. I could barely function. I lost all sensibilities. I kept thinking, *Gabriel is disturbed and unstable. We are in trouble. He could snap again and kill us all.*

The police eventually showed up that night after a relative alerted them. Gabriel had a gun by his pillow and told Lisa that if the police came into his house there would be a shoot-out. Lisa, thankful that Gabriel was passed out drunk upstairs, met the officers at the door. She quietly asked them to come back in the morning to speak with him, as he was asleep upstairs. The police asked if there were guns in the house. All she could think about was Gabriel's last words, *shoot-out.* She lied, "No," trying to reassure them—and herself—that everything was fine.

They left a contact card and said they'd return in the morning to speak with him.

There were countless times we made plans to visit and at the last minute—sometimes we were already on the highway—when Lisa would call me apologetically with an excuse to cancel. Only later did we learn Lisa lied because Gabriel threatened to make things miserable for everyone, and she would pay the consequences later.

He'd say, "Tell them not to come; I'm not in the mood."

"Gabriel, I can't cancel again," she pleaded.

"I'm telling you to cancel. If you don't, I'm turning off the water and I'm leaving. You can stay up here and freeze," he threatened.

Beyond our weekend socials, we would also vacation with them in the Caribbean or Mexico. Lisa and I would spend the day together at the pool and on the beach, while the boys would explore the island. We tended to do our own thing through the day, and then catch up later in the evening. Lisa told me Gabriel preferred eating at the buffets because of the variety of food they had, and he could eat as much as he wanted. This one time they agreed to join us for supper at an à la carte.

We were waiting at the restaurant when they finally walked in.

"What took you so long?" I asked them.

Neither answered right away, but Lisa's facial expression gave it away, before adding, "Gabriel wanted to check out the buffet."

"Oh, Gabriel. You ate? Are you even hungry anymore?" I asked slyly.

I must have embarrassed him, as the table went silent. Without saying anything, Gabriel just got up and left. Lisa tried to make it OK, apologized for him, and followed him out, mouthing, "I'm sorry."

We ended up eating alone that night. "Ridiculous," I said. "He is so weird. Who does that? I wish she would have just let him go. She probably won't get to eat tonight."

The next day, we did our own thing until Lisa joined us at the pool. "Where's Gabe?" I asked.

"He's up in the room on his computer."

Gabriel stayed there the entire day. There was never one vacation we took together that his odd behaviour didn't show up. We just got used to it. It was infuriating at times, but Lisa put up with it and I learned to ignore it.

As we grew older, Lisa and I pictured enjoying our retirement years together. As close sisters, we envisioned owning land and building homes near each other. We'd create a small community of family just as we had experienced on Quarry Road. We fantasized how fun it would be. We would be safe, and able to support each other in our older years. We could pass our family land and traditions onto our children and generations to come.

I ran the idea by our other siblings, but they weren't interested: "No, are you crazy? I'm not going near him," said one. By now, most of our family had minimal contact with Gabriel, as he rarely socialized at our annual gatherings. Janice and I spent the most time with Lisa and Gabriel as a couple.

In 2018, I bought a piece of land next to the warehouse in Portapique. I was leery given Gabriel was too unpredictable to be around full time but, what could I do? Lisa wasn't going anywhere. At least I'd be close and could ensure her safety. I couldn't have been more wrong.

JANICE:

My relationship with Gabriel was that of a brother/sister: a love-hate dynamic. I knew he respected me and, dare I say, loved me like a sister as well. Lisa and I are a lot alike in many ways, being only one year apart. As complicated as Lisa's relationship was with Gabriel, so too was mine. Despite all his insufferable behaviour, there were seeds of decency that I chose to focus on. To maintain a relationship with my sister, I learned to temper my expectations and support Lisa as best I could.

As best friends, I shared my financial struggles with Lisa. My former home was old and required extensive renovations. When Lisa told Gabriel, he helped me out without any request for compensation. Gabriel was an incredible carpenter; he had every tool you can name. I was grateful. I felt genuine kindness from him many times. He would step up like a brother, never asking for anything in return. That meant a lot to me, especially as we were having financial difficulties at the time.

Lisa told me intimate details of their relationship—the good, the bad, and the disturbing. The stories of abuse he suffered as a child at the hands of his parents tore at my maternal heart. How could anyone hurt a child like that? This gave way to my overwhelming empathy for that broken part of him. I leaned on my sisters for everything, and I could not imagine experiencing what he did without a support system. I wanted desperately for him to get help, and always suggested therapy and working through his trauma. But it fell on deaf ears. He'd always say he's smarter than psychologists; he had it all figured out. He did take up Transcendental Meditation at one point, but like everything he did, he'd do it hard for months then he'd move on to something else. Gabriel lived in the extremes.

Like Maureen, I never witnessed his direct physical abuse. I saw him groping and grabbing her body as if she was a piece of meat. It was disgusting. I had to bite my tongue as Lisa's death stare stifled my words. I remember being so angry that she was putting up with his crap. I don't know who I hated more at that moment, him for being so openly vulgar or Lisa for not standing up to him.

There were other times I refused to be silenced. Gabriel and I would get into some volatile confrontations. We'd have get-togethers at the warehouse on the weekends, where we'd dance, drink, and have deep conversations about life. The topics were intense and real: abuse, addiction, money, relationships. I'd ask why he had such a need for excess; why he needed more of everything? And why were they so obsessively jealous toward each other? Gabriel's pride meant he always wanted bigger and better. He was never physical with me, but at times, if I'm honest, some of our exchanges did unsettle me.

Lisa despised our fighting because she couldn't predict how Gabriel might react.

"Would you guys just stop, please?" she begged. "Just drop it!"

She would tremble and almost hyperventilate, trying to redirect us. Lisa frantically wanted to maintain the peace. She would pull me aside: "Janice, please stop. I know how Gabriel can be. You are getting him revved up and he could snap at any time. I know what I can get away with, you don't." I could feel her fear but still had no idea the depths of her panic.

I backed off.

JANICE AND MAUREEN:

One of our biggest strategies for coping became compartmentalization. We'd focus on the present and the things we could control. Everything else got put aside, pushed down, or blocked it from her memory. There were times when Lisa was in Dartmouth, but we didn't hear from her. She normally reached out daily, so when she fell silent our spidey-senses urged us to check in with an impromptu visit.

As we suspected, something was up. We knew Lisa covered up for him. At times, Lisa complained her body ached and she favoured her arm or leg or back. She'd reference being accident-prone, saying she banged into something; any excuse not to tell the truth. We knew what was really happening—and she knew that we knew. Regardless, she wasn't prepared to leave him, so what could we do? We ended up coping as she did, clinging to the good days and hoping that things would get better. We understood it was fear-based, but beyond that, Lisa was determined to love the good parts of Gabriel. Her heart believed that loving him unconditionally would eventually mend his brokenness.

But Gabriel's internal madness mutated into an evil we didn't want to see. We didn't trust him. We knew to our core that if he couldn't have her, no one else would. For the sake of maintaining contact with our beloved sister, we tolerated him, all the while fearing the worst. Gabriel could be a ticking time bomb and Lisa justly feared him. We truly believed we were going to bury our sister one day. It is gut-wrenching to think about how Lisa suffered his iron fists all alone. Truth is, we all suffered his tyranny. Even now, thinking about what we could have done differently, our fear petrifies us.

9

Turning Point

IN THE SUMMER of 2018, my sisters and I saw something in Gabriel we had never seen before. Gabriel had been struggling with his drinking. He was generally fit and strong. We both ate well. We craved salads and fruit and although Gabriel didn't exercise, he was extremely active. He never stopped moving. I grew worried when he complained of fatigue. He just wasn't himself. I thought he was experiencing man-o-pause. I'd been perimenopausal for years, so I got it. It is hard getting older. I thought it was a phase or his new normal, but it got worse. He almost seemed depressed. He lost interest in work, projects, and most alarmingly, sex. I knew then, something was definitely wrong.

I convinced him to see a doctor, who sent him for blood tests. The results concerned us. After years of excessive drinking, his liver had suffered. The doctor suggested a strict diet and urged him to give up alcohol. He'd often go on health kicks, feel good, but eventually return to old habits. I think this time it scared him. Perhaps he had gone too far. He gave up alcohol before, and he was much easier to live with when he got sober. His moods got better, and he became less aggressive.

Gabriel enjoyed physical work, but in the last few years he found it harder. He wasn't old, but the reality of aging affected him. He got me to buy particular bread, milk, nuts, fruits, vitamins, tonics—anything and everything toting improved liver function. The sprouted bread alone cost $12 a loaf. It didn't matter to him, as long as it was healthy. When Gabriel had a goal, he would research what was needed and then execute it to the extreme.

As his fiftieth birthday in July approached, I wanted to have something special for him. He had a rough year health-wise, and I hoped a birthday party could help put that behind him. But who to invite? The problem was that he didn't have many friends in Nova Scotia, and he wasn't talking to most of his family.

His closest buddies lived in Houlton, Maine. Gabriel visited the States more often than I did, but together we drove down to visit his friends several times a year, and more so recently. The first time I met Sean Conlogue, Gabriel took me shopping in Maine. He had just bought a Ford F150 and Sean invited us to stay at his childhood home. He made us feel so welcome.

Sean liked guns, so he and Gabriel would go to firearms shows and I would go shopping with his neighbourhood friend, Angel. We would all go to the local Elks Lodge and have drinks. Gabriel did everything for Sean. He renovated his two-storey home, mowed his lawn, and did anything else he needed. Sean gave him a house key; he trusted him that much. For someone so private, it told me a lot about their relationship.

When we were there, I socialized and bonded with Sean, Angel, and her partner. I really liked Angel, yet there was something I didn't quite trust about her. I found her overly flirtatious for someone in a long-term relationship. I didn't like it, but it seemed to be part of her friendly nature and her man didn't seem to be concerned. They were all thrilled to come to Nova Scotia to surprise Gabriel.

Apart from Janice, Maureen, and Stephanie, I didn't think anyone else from my family would have shown up if it was a birthday party just for Gabriel. Maureen thought of a way we could celebrate his birthday by combining it with a family summer kickoff with my other sisters and brothers.

We all watched the television show *Survivor* and usually got together as a family on Canada Day. It took us months of planning, but we created our very own "Family Survivor." We even made a trophy for the winner. We developed group and individual games so there was something for everyone. The games included sack races, obstacle courses, water balloons/egg tosses, chugging games, and other silly activities. We organized the weekend as a family summer social, but the real reason was to celebrate Gabriel turning fifty.

Unbeknownst to me, Maureen secretly coordinated with Gabriel a surprise fiftieth for me at the same time. Gabriel's July birthday was close to mine in August, so it was the perfect ruse for turning the weekend bash into a double birthday celebration.

As Maureen and I elaborately planned a *Survivor* weekend, she worked with Gabriel on my surprise party. This would be the first time Sean and Angel came to Nova Scotia and stayed at our cottage. We had some guests sleep in our warehouse bedrooms, and I booked accommodations for everyone else to stay in local Airbnbs for the weekend. Everyone was within walking distance of the festivities. It didn't cost them anything. They could relax and drink without worry. We set up outdoor tents for shade, had a barbecue and lobster feast, and turned the warehouse into a cool nightclub with its custom bar, affectionately named Lisa's Bar.

Our warehouse looked more like a pub. Gabriel bought the bar, stools, lights, and even the steel sink from a Montana's Restaurant near our home that had recently been renovated. But there were notable decorations that stood out: stuffed buffalo and moose heads. Half of the main floor was a shrine to Gabriel's collection of motorcycles, country antiques, and RCMP memorabilia, including a replica police car. At the time, he said he wanted the car to be a tribute to fallen officers.

I hired a DJ who played all our favourites from the loft above the dance floor. Strings of patio lights criss-crossed the length of the room and strobes matched the beat of the music. It was a night to remember.

It worked like a charm. Neither of us had any idea of the other's surprise. My whole family was in on it. I also made calls to his Uncle Chris in British Columbia, friends from Cape Breton, and a few locals to join us in Portapique. They all came. Some even changed their plans to be there for Gabriel. Combined with all my family members, we were going to make incredible memories. I could not wait to see Gabriel's face when he realized the party was actually for him.

The moment Gabriel walked into the cottage, he looked stunned by the crowd and decorations. It was like his brain couldn't process what was happening. When Sean and Angel popped out of the crowd and hooted, "Surprise!" he stood frozen in disbelief. His nervous grin turned to a genuine smile as everyone surrounded him with hugs and well wishes. "I'm speechless," he kept repeating, as the warmth of the moment flushed his cheeks and he welled up.

He nervously scratched his arms as his eyes scouted the room and its happy guests, then he choked up. No one had ever planned anything like that for him in his life. His parents didn't have any childhood birthday parties, so he found this overwhelming as he moved from one person to another, greeting them with hugs and handshakes, *This is for me?* His smile grew wider as he made his way through the procession of people ending in the kitchen. I had a birthday T-shirt designed for him, and all the guests wrote messages as a keepsake.

After the big reveal for Gabriel, we gathered items, and all set out to the warehouse. I had no clue that I was about to be surprised as well. Maureen arranged for my best friend Denise to pick up my birthday cake and deliver it to me. It wasn't until Denise came from the back room carrying a beautifully flowered cake of buttercream swirls that I realized the party was for me too. I bawled. We had two of everything: cakes, gifts, decorations, and presentations. The warehouse filled with laughter, and for that day I experienced life as it should be, as I dreamed it could be with Gabriel. For the first time, I felt Gabriel was part of the Banfield clan.

* * *

A year later in 2019, we talked about that weekend. We listened to some music and danced together. Gabriel seemed melancholy. "What's wrong? Are you OK?"

His lips quivered but he didn't answer.

I asked again, "Gabriel, what's wrong?"

"I wish I could tell you."

"What Gabriel? You're scaring me. Are you sick?"

"I just wish I could share everything that goes on in my head. I'm thinking all the time, you know. You are such a good person, Lisa. I'm not like you."

"What are you talking about?" I asked but I dreaded his response. "Gabriel, you are a good person, too. You help a lot of people," I reminded him. He remained quiet.

I could barely get out the words. He was scaring me, "Gabriel, are you dying?"

"No, but I know when I'm going to die."

"Gabriel, stop! Nobody knows that."

"I do," he said pitifully. "I'm going out with a bang."

Thinking he was talking about suicide, I pulled away. "Gabriel, stop. I don't like this." Any time he talked like that, I would just shut him down or walk away. I motioned to leave.

"Don't go. I'll stop." He gently pulled me back.

After a brief silence, I squeezed him tighter. "It will be OK," I told him. "Don't talk like that. It will be OK."

But it wasn't.

***

Christmas time was always triggering for Gabriel. I think that is why he preferred to stay up at the cottage while I visited my family. The compromise worked for us. I got to celebrate with my entire family then I'd travel to Portapique so Gabriel and I could celebrate our own quiet Christmas. That December, I had spent days decorating the tree and transforming our log home into a wonderland of lights, candles, and evergreen boughs. The seasonal music, cinnamon scents, and colourful glowing lights made for a magical time.

But I knew this blissful time would end as it always did. I waited, attuned to any indication that he was going to lose it, but there'd be no rhyme or reason, no logical antecedent. While I'd grown accustomed to Gabriel's beatings after almost two decades together, every time he attacked me, I was surprised.

Something changed for me when I turned fifty. I found an inner strength that gave me voice: "Gabriel, I'm getting too old for this. My body can't take it anymore." Instead of trying to placate him, I spoke my truth. "I didn't do anything to you. I've always been there for you. I have loved you unconditionally and I don't deserve to be treated like this. I am telling you, now, if you ever hit me again, I will leave and I will never come back. I'm done living like this."

10

Isolation

FIVE WEEKS BEFORE

GABRIEL'S DREAM CAME true. On March 10, 2020, he had me all to himself. We had shut down our denture business and were moving out of the city just days before the first COVID-19 cases were confirmed in Nova Scotia.[2] Our coastal province had kept the deadly virus at bay through strict public health protocols. But it was just a matter of time, so we fled like other people who could escape the virus and find refuge at their cottages. We would hunker down in Portapique, surrounded by nature and the sea; there we would be safe from catching the virus.

It would be very different for us, as I'd only spent weekends in Portapique, and never weeks at a time. I was too afraid to stay there by myself. I did like the idea of retreating to the peacefulness of the countryside. Now in our fifties, we had planned to move here permanently, and our Dartmouth home/clinic had a private offer pending. It made sense to try living at our cottage and I felt grateful we had that option.

"Lisa, I can't see us going back home until they find a cure or an antidote for COVID," Gabriel said.

"Do you think we will get sick of each other 24/7?" I asked, half-joking. Things felt more stable between us, so I tried to be optimistic. This would be a semi-retirement test for us.

"It'll be great. You can do your walks, and I'll go over to the warehouse," he said convincingly. "You know me—I can keep myself busy with lots of things."

Gabriel began to track every news channel as his paranoia about COVID intensified. He told me to put a "No Visitors" sign on the front door of the cottage and the warehouse. Within five days, N.S. Public Health confirmed three cases were brought into the province by people travelling: a man in his fifties, a woman in her sixties, and a young man in his thirties, all had the virus. By the end of that week, the federal government ordered an end to all non-essential travel outside Canada, and those returning home had to self-isolate for two weeks.

I loved our cottage, but I felt isolated in Portapique without my family. The pandemic shut down everyone's world, including mine. Except for the obvious stress of circumstances, Gabriel was enjoying not having to compete for my attention. "You know, if this is retirement, I'm loving it," he told me one morning.

Thankfully, FaceTime allowed me to talk to my family. There is no way I could have stayed at the cottage without that technology. The only way I could see my sisters in person during the next few weeks was when I squeezed in a short visit while doing an errand run to the city to buy things or get the mail from the Dartmouth clinic.

Gabriel wanted me to rush back: "Make sure you just go there and come right back. I don't want you visiting your family. If you bring that virus back to me, you will regret it."

Despite his warning, I made sure they weren't symptomatic and saw them briefly. I know I risked contracting the virus, but I needed to see my family. I missed them.

As the weeks passed, the government closed more public places, and I watched Gabriel struggle with the pandemic hysteria. Many of the things Gabriel predicted seemed to come true. His already abnormal behaviour became more bizarre. Since we built the cottage, Gabriel kept a fireproof safe there. We had collected over $200,000 in it with thousands more in an orange tin at the warehouse. I know that for many people, this is hard to believe: Who keeps that kind of cash on hand? But after knowing him for nineteen years, Gabriel trusted no one and was extremely paranoid of government and banking institutions. This is how he protected our money. It was much the same as people did years ago, socking cash away under a mattress or in their freezer.

Within weeks of arriving in Portapique, Gabriel started worrying our savings were at risk. He read the predictions that the federal government may close all institutions or the banks would collapse, leaving our money out of reach. That is why he held accounts with most of the major Canadian banks, and even a Chase Manhattan Bank account in Maine. He told me banks would only insure a maximum amount, and he always wanted access to our funds if we needed them. Politics played into his deteriorating logic. Gabriel didn't trust Prime Minister Justin Trudeau at all. "Interventionist," he would complain, "especially with the vaccine." Gabriel favoured American President Donald Trump's individual-rights approach to the pandemic.

By the end of March, Gabriel wanted to withdraw all our money out of the banks. "I'd feel better if it was buried in our backyard. I'm taking it out and when I feel more secure about the banks, I'll put it back in the bank," he told me casually over breakfast.

Once his mind was made up, he was on a mission, and I felt that familiar unease creep in as I watched him detail his plan. I wanted to question him more, but as always I opted to keep the peace and just follow his lead. He used my cellphone to call the CIBC, where we had the most saved up, to liquidate the investments. He put it on speakerphone as he tried to arrange an appointment to pick up the money accounts. They seemed to stall or discourage him, because it was such a large amount. Then they advised he'd have to pick it up from a Brink's depot in Dartmouth, arranged by them. Later, conspiracy theorists believed getting so much cash at Brink's rather than a bank was proof that Gabriel might have worked undercover for the police and was being paid for providing them information. The truth is Gabriel just did what the bank directed him to do. No one I knew ever had to do something that formal, but no one I knew was withdrawing close to half a million dollars in cash either.

When I told Maureen what we were doing, she was scared for me and insisted on following us to be sure nothing sketchy happened. "I am not comfortable with you travelling with that cash," Maureen said.

On March 30, we drove to pick up $475,000, cash bundled in $100 bills. I followed Gabriel in our truck. He told me to call the police if anyone tried to rob him. Maureen was to meet us at Tim Hortons in Dartmouth. When we got to the depot, a Brink's driver gave Gabriel the cash in a duffel bag that he locked in his trunk. Maureen followed behind us for half an hour, watching out for suspicious cars, but didn't notice anything unusual. By the time we reached the Halifax airport turnoff, twenty minutes outside the city, she turned around.

Once we were back in Portapique, Gabriel told me to collect all the other cash in the cottage and add it to what we had brought from Dartmouth that day. He took a bath while I counted the money on the bed. When he came out of the bathroom, I looked at him. Like out of a movie, we had $750,000 stacked on the bed. He stuffed it in an oversized Cabela's canvas bag.

The next morning, as we ate breakfast, he talked about the plan as if nothing was unusual about burying money in our yard. He had it all figured out, a scheme so unreal I couldn't make it up.

Gabriel had built our front deck to include a concrete slab that had a built-in hatch. You wouldn't notice it unless you knew about it. The trap door allowed us to lower a ladder to the ground below and bury the money. To further conceal the duffel bag of money, Gabriel put it in a garbage bag and covered it.

"It will be safe here," he said. "If something ever happens to me, you're the only one who will know where it is."

***

During the next several weeks, Gabriel didn't sleep well and often skipped meals. One night, I woke up to pee at 2 a.m. and saw a light on in his bedroom. As I tiptoed closer to see what he was doing, I heard Trump's voice talking about COVID and the news commentators warning listeners that the world would never be the same. It sounded so catastrophic; no wonder people were scared. I returned to my bedroom without saying a word.

With so much time on his hands, every day, for hours on end, he listened to negative predictions spewing doomsday from CNN and other news outlets. Gabriel had started ranting more and more about the world ending. Finally, I'd had enough.

"Why don't you take a break from that? Listen to it for an hour and breathe, look at something positive other than these negative messages all the time," I urged him. "Why don't you go to the warehouse and do some work? That will take your mind off things."

"Lisa, it's good to know what's going on in the world," he insisted.

"I don't want to even talk about Donald Trump; we're on two different pages," I would say, trying to avoid an argument. "The local updates from the premier and Chief Medical Officer Dr. Strang is all I need to hear," I countered.

The negative talk drained me, so I would go for my walks and listen to my spiritual podcasts. One April morning I returned home to find him still in bed.

"Are you going to get up?" I asked him.

"I just don't have the umph," he said.

I worried, but didn't know how to shake him out of it. I couldn't stand listening to his paranoia and negativity made worse when talking to his American friend Sean and his buddy Leonard, a fellow denturist in Cape Breton. As much as I liked Leonard, he could be very negative too. They were feeding off each other and venting about the mounting deaths due to COVID. Because of that, I started ignoring my cellphone when I saw it was Leonard. One night we were at the warehouse, and I forgot I had my ringer turned on. Gabriel picked it up and they started talking on speakerphone so I could hear.

"Enough about this negative stuff. Leonard, do you ever watch Joel Osteen? You need to watch him. It's uplifting; it's something positive instead of dwelling on the negative," I said. "Osteen has many life-affirming videos I watch for inspiration. I think you'd really like him."

By now, the government had declared a provincial state of emergency to help contain the spread of COVID. Beaches and parks closed. We were ordered to social distance or face fines of $1,000 and could only leave home for essential items like food or gas. One morning, Gabriel asked me to do a food run.

"Lisa, we have to stock up on food, so that we have everything we need."

During my weekly trips to Costco in Dartmouth, he wanted me to buy extra canned goods, flour, rice, water, and meat. We had six extra freezers at the warehouse to stockpile the food. It seemed over the top to me, but that is what it was like living with Gabriel.

"Gabriel, we're not going to be out of food and the grocery stores are not going to shut down."

"It's just a matter of time," he said. "I want lots of gas, food—everything we need. It's just you and me in this world, so I want to make sure we get the stuff while we can."

He waited until the gas prices dropped, as they are typically reset at midnight on Thursdays in Nova Scotia—and with COVID they were at an all-time low. On April 11, Gabriel loaded two blue forty-gallon buckets plus more than a dozen of our jerry cans onto his trailer and hitched it to our truck. We drove to the gas station in Masstown, about twenty minutes away. He filled them all and paid about $600. He seemed relieved to get that done, but the more he watched TV and read stuff on the internet, the more desperate he got.

"I know when I'm going to die." This was the second time he said that to me.

"Nobody knows when they're going to die, Gabriel."

Over the years he would say he was not afraid of dying. He had embalmed people as he worked as a funeral director, and it did not phase him. It freaked me out. When he'd get into one of those moods, I'd just change the topic. I did not want to listen to his crazy talk.

As the pandemic worsened, he said we should move over to the warehouse soon, because it would be safer. The warehouse did not have as many windows, he said; it was built more like a fortress. Its heavy steel doors and locks, fortified by layers of tin-panelled sheets, made it a perfect bunker from possible intruders.

Gabriel always owned guns; he loved them and collected many throughout his life. Although I feared guns, Gabriel insisted on having them so he could protect us. He kept moving them to different places in the house and warehouse. I didn't want to know where he put them. I was just thankful not to have them around me: out-of-sight, out-of-mind, kind of thing. Dad and some other family members hunted, but the girls never bothered with them. I had no idea at that time you required a firearms license to own guns, even hunting rifles. Many times Gabriel wanted to buy me a little pistol to keep in my purse. "I don't want a gun," I told him. "That will never happen."

Gabriel told me that Sean told him that you can't even get guns there anymore and to get as much ammunition as you can because if something happened, people needed to defend themselves. The United States seemed to be getting more extreme, and Gabriel was listening to all of it with keen interest. On my last trip to Dartmouth, he asked me to get more bullets for him. "Why do you need more bullets? You have lots of bullets. You don't need anymore."

"I just want them, Lisa. I told you things are getting bad. Get them."

I wanted him off my back, so I asked my brother and my brother-in-law who were hunters if they would get them for Gabriel.

Janice grilled me on the phone. "Why is he getting you to do that?"

"You know what he's like—he wants to be prepared; he's paranoid, thinking people are going to get desperate and try to take our stuff," I told her. To me it was Gabriel trying to be in control yet again. I prayed our upcoming anniversary would offer a reset from his obsessive paranoia about the pandemic. I could not have been more wrong.

PART III

Tribulation

I thought I could heal him if I loved him enough.

11

Our Nineteenth Anniversary

SATURDAY, APRIL 18, 2020

The what ifs still haunt me. What if I didn't escape to the woods, would those innocent people still be alive? To this day I struggle with survivor guilt, and probably always will.

ON APRIL 18, 2020, I woke up to a beautiful spring morning. The sun beckoned me to get moving. I could get my morning walk in before noon.

Because COVID kept us isolated from other people, on Sundays my sisters and I played our own version of bingo over FaceTime. We'd share a laugh, teasing each other about who would win. We only played for ten bucks, but we had a building jackpot, so once a month one of us got a chance at $50.

"Gabriel, I was thinking we could celebrate our anniversary today because tomorrow we have our family bingo," I suggested, greeting him with a morning kiss.

Catching up on the news on his laptop, Gabriel agreed. We decided to go for a ride later and I would pack us lunch. I made his favourite breakfast then got ready for my walk. He went back to bed to finish his morning news, and I headed out.

I valued my alone time, especially amid nature. I meandered along the muddy Bay of Fundy banks as the sun sparkled further out on the Atlantic Ocean. I felt blessed. I was grateful we had this beautiful place to enjoy. I savoured the peaceful time to myself and used the privacy to catch up with family and friends. I recited prayers and listened to my music and positive affirmations.

I would never have imagined it would be my last stroll here.

When I returned to the cottage, I packed some snacks so we could stop for a picnic somewhere. We jumped in the Jeep for a drive.

"Where do you want to go?" Gabriel asked me.

"Wherever—doesn't matter to me," I said. "It's so nice out; it's a perfect day for a country drive."

"OK, let's take the dirt back roads," he suggested.

We drove for an hour, and the roads were definitely remote; some transitioned to gravel then back to asphalt but it was quietly beautiful. We came upon an area of untouched lakes and streams. It wasn't unusual to explore back roads, as we had done it for years during our time in Colchester County. Sometimes we'd take the side-by-side and spend the day trekking to the beach or through the vast farmlands of Bass River. Gabriel knew the woods as if he was born there. Half the time, I had no idea where we were, but it was always picturesque and peaceful.

Gabriel was quieter than usual. He seemed preoccupied. We didn't reminisce or talk about our anniversary, which saddened me.

I noticed a huge lake to the right and said, "Where are we?"

When Gabriel casually said Sutherland Lake, I flinched. But he kept driving as if he hadn't remembered what happened the last time I was here.

What? Are you serious? I thought. *You are taking me to the first place you abused me?* Not a happy memory, especially on our anniversary.

Disturbing flashbacks filled my mind. I stared out the window. I didn't say anything, as he rambled on about the surroundings.

As we pulled onto the main highway, Gabriel pointed up a hill to a penitentiary. "I'd never survive there. My uncle served time there, but I would never last in prison," he commented. It was such a random thing to say, but I was still lost in my own thoughts and not really listening to him.

I wanted to stop for a picnic lunch, but he wasn't interested. He just wanted to keep driving. Instead of pushing it, I fed him grapes and watermelon from the passenger side. Then we pulled into the Debert Diefenbunker. Gabriel was fascinated by this spot. Designed and built at the height of the Cold War, the two-storey, 64-square-foot bunker was built to serve as a regional military headquarters in the event of a nuclear attack.[3] He'd shown me it years ago when he thought about trying to buy part of the land from the federal government. It meant nothing to me. *Can we just move on from here,* I thought. *I'm getting bored.*

This was not the romantic day I'd hoped for, and it was getting late. We'd been driving for several hours now. By mid-afternoon, as we headed toward home Gabriel recognized the house of a denturist colleague he knew. He pulled the Jeep into the driveway and called the guy on my cellphone. By now, I'm thinking, *What are we doing now? Why are we visiting a denturist on our special day?*

The whole day felt weird. I just wanted to go home; I was done.

The guy came out and seemed happy to see Gabriel. I had never met him before.

"Oh, you got an eighteen-year-old with you, do you?" the friend said, teasing me.

"You're sweet. Thank you."

They started joking around about dentures. I sat there and eventually leaned over and said, "OK, Gabriel, let's go. I don't want to stay here and talk about stupid teeth."

We left shortly after and picked up pizza and beer to bring home.

We pulled into the warehouse around supper time and Gabriel washed the Jeep from our day's ride. I made my way through the woods to the cottage to change and gather a few things for our night's celebration. Hopefully it would be more romantic than the day had been.

When I returned to the warehouse, Gabriel turned the music on, and we danced a bit as we drank. I made my Caesar the way I liked it, while Gabriel drank his beers. We talked about maybe buying another wooded lot between our cottage and the warehouse. Full retirement wasn't far off, and we still hoped that some of my family would move here too. "If you build it, they will come," I'd hoped.

At 6 p.m., I got my phone and took a selfie of us. I sent it to Janice with the caption: "Happy 19th Together." I tried to FaceTime Sean to say hi, but Gabriel said he wasn't in the mood. I quickly hung up before he answered. Gabriel must have still been out of sorts, because we'd call Sean every night from the warehouse. I wasn't sure why he was acting so strange. Sean ended up calling us back and apologized for missing our call. Once they started talking, Gabriel seemed fine.

Because of the COVID border lockdowns, we hadn't seen Sean or Angel for a while. I missed our visits to Maine, where we hung out and shopped for bargains. Sean got emotional, as he too reminisced with us. "I love you guys," he said. "Same," said Gabriel, who was starting to feel his liquor.

We FaceTimed Angel next. After catching up, I told her next year would be our twentieth anniversary together, so we were planning a commitment ceremony. Not a wedding, I clarified. We weren't getting married because Gabriel didn't want to get married again, but we wanted to commit to each other in a formal way. We'd write our own vows and share them with everyone we loved.

Gabriel had my phone and was walking into the back room when I heard my friend Angel say to him, "Don't do it."

I couldn't believe she said that to him. It pissed me off. *Why would she say such a thing?*

I grabbed the phone from him, "Why would you say that?" I asked her.

"I didn't mean it that way," she started.

"I'm letting you go, Angel," and I hung up, upset.

Realizing the night wasn't what I thought it would be, I told Gabriel, "I'm done; I'm going to the cottage."

"Really, Lisa?" he said sarcastically. "Don't be so sensitive. She was only joking."

Tired from a disappointing day, I left, dragging myself through the path in the woods to our cottage. As I walked, I thought twice about how I'd acted. I realized I was angrier at Angel than Gabriel, so I turned back to apologize to him.

Gabriel was downing another beer when I walked into the warehouse. I attempted my usual, "I'm sorry, let's start over," but I barely got out the words, "I was mad at Angel, not you."

When he scowled at me. "You always have to ruin everything."

"I didn't, Gabriel. She shouldn't have said that. I'm letting it go tonight but the next time we go down there, I'm having a conversation with her."

Then he turned to me in a rage, "You're such a bitch. Why do you have to ruin everything?" he yelled at me.

He continued to spew nasty names and insults at me, then he crossed the line. I knew at this point nothing good was going to come of this night. "I don't need to hear this; I didn't do anything. I got pissed off, but I don't deserve what you're dishing out right now, so I'm leaving."

I left the warehouse and made my way through the trail back to the cottage for the night.

I went to bed. *Some anniversary.*

12

The First Victim

SATURDAY EVENING, APRIL 18, 2020

I DON'T KNOW how long I was in bed when I heard him return from the warehouse. I heard a weird whooshing sound. *What was he doing?* I pretended to be asleep when Gabriel opened my door. If I ignored him, maybe he would just leave me alone. But he didn't. He stood over my bed and began screaming at me:

"Get up!" He ripped off the blanket, exposing my naked body. I was alarmed, but tried once again to redirect him as I pulled the covers back up and told him to go to bed. This time he persisted and kept yelling at me to get up. He was in a mood and wanted to fight. This was not going to be good. Without warning, he took my laptop from my bed stand and smashed it on the floor.

"Gabriel, what are you doing?" I screamed.

Furious I hadn't moved as he commanded, he grabbed my cellphone and did the same thing, but this time crushed it under the weight of his boot.

Something within him snapped.

He yanked the blankets off me and grabbed me by the hair, forcing me to the floor. He got on top of me and started choking me.

My instincts took over and I tried to stay calm, "Gabriel, it's OK. I'm sorry."

"Get up," he ordered me, "I'm done."

I kept trying to talk him down. "Gabriel, what's wrong? What's happening?"

He wasn't having any of it.

"Oh, you stubborn bitch. You got a little Beulah and Gilly in you." He pulled me up by my hair. I tried cradling my head to ease the excruciating tension on my scalp.

As I stood up, he kicked me in the stomach, sending me backward onto the corner post of my bed. The solid log post of the Amish pine frame offered no flex as I felt and heard my lower back crack. I dropped to the floor, wincing in pain. I lost my breath. Stunned, I froze. I wanted the beating to stop.

"Get up," he barked at me.

I tried, but it was so painful. Before he could hit me again, I found my inner strength and used the bedpost to get up as he demanded.

Still naked, I braced myself before he'd hit me again.

"Get dressed," he yelled. He opened my closet door.

I grabbed whatever I could get on quickly, a pair of tights and a thin black top.

"Let me get my purse? I need my purse."

"You don't need your purse," he yelled, grabbing me by the right wrist. He tied something around it. I think it was from a bathrobe belt in my closet. I'm not sure, but it was a soft material. I couldn't think clearly or process what was happening.

"Let's not forget my gun. I need my gun," he said in a calm, matter-of-fact way.

He dragged me around the house. We went through the kitchen to his bedroom. "Be careful. It's slippery," I heard him say.

Are you kidding me? I thought. *You just beat the shit out of me and now you're worried I might slip?*

He walked past the open safe that contained $60,000, without taking any of it. He was in his own zone as he entered his bedroom. He grabbed his black handgun tucked in a nook of the adjoining sunroom. We walked down to the landing by the front door, where he picked up a jerry can of gas and threw it into our sunken living room. I put my bare feet into sneakers when, in a calm, eerie robot state, he said, "Turn around."

And as I did, flames erupted. It was surreal.

I knew he had lost his mind. Gabriel would never damage the home he took so much pride in creating. I had to get free; I had to run.

Still tethered by the robe belt or whatever it was, we moved from our deck to the driveway. He doused our white decommissioned car with gasoline but didn't light it.

Instead of screaming at him, I tried to stay calm and offered him a way out. "Gabriel, it's OK," I said soothingly, even though it was anything but OK. "Gabriel, I'll tell them I accidentally started the fire. I will take the blame. It will be OK. Please, please Gabriel, don't do this."

"It is too late; you will never look at me the same way," he said.

He pulled me to the road as the flames engulfed our home. I dug my heels into the gravel, trying to slow his pace.

"Gabriel, please don't do this. We can get through this," I pleaded.

"It's too late, Lisa. You told me if I ever hit you again, you'd leave. I'm done."

I dropped to the ground and tried to kick him away. He ripped my sneakers off, then threw them in opposite directions on the road. "You can't run now, you little bitch."

I didn't know how to stop him; he'd gone too far. I needed help.

"At the end of the night, I'm gonna die," he said coldly. "You won't die, as long as you don't run away from me."

His eyes darkened. Stark and distant, I didn't see Gabriel anymore. It was like there was no light in them. Forcing me to my bare feet, he dragged me across the road to the entrance of the woods. I cried out in pain.

On the path back to our warehouse, adrenaline kicked in. I thought if I could just get out of my unzipped coat and run, I could escape. He wanted me to go in front of him. I knew this path as well as him, but in the dark I struggled to get my bearings.

I reacted instinctively, shifting my shoulder, I got out of my coat and fled. I couldn't see anything; I tripped over some kind of root. I tried to hide, but he had a flashlight so he found me instantly and grabbed me.

My stomach churned as he confirmed my worst nightmare. *He's going to kill my family*. My back throbbed. He ignored my moans as he thrust me forward. I didn't cry. I stayed silent so as not to anger him further.

As soon as we came to the driveway, he released me. "Don't move." His eyes said it all.

I watched in horror. He poured gasoline on all our cars, the white Ford F-150, and his backhoe. He calmly unlocked all the dead bolts and opened the warehouse doors.

Once we were inside, he grabbed a set of handcuffs from behind the bar. "Give me your hands."

"Gabriel, you don't have to do this, please," I begged.

He cuffed my left wrist. "Give me your other wrist."

He was on a mission and couldn't be stopped. "We're going to burn down the Dartmouth clinic and then we're going to Maureen's."

Dear God. If he's going to kill my family, just kill me, now. I dropped to my knees and covered my face with my hands. A shot rang in my ears. I never heard a gunshot up close. It ricocheted off the cement to the right of me.

"Give me your other hand," he demanded.

"Gabriel, please, don't," I said hysterically.

"I'm not going to tell you again. Give me your other hand."

Another blast hit the floor on the left side of me. Terrified that my head would be his next target, my entire body numbed. I lost hope.

Perhaps exasperated by my refusal to move, Gabriel grabbed my arm and pushed me into the backseat of the replica police cruiser, slamming the car door as he walked away.

He tossed guns onto the front-seat passenger side. I panicked. *I'm trapped.*

At least I had use of my hands, but I needed these cuffs off. I struggled to free my left wrist without success. There were no door handles in the back seat, so I kicked at the partition to the front seat. I kept kicking with my bare feet while he was out of sight. The Plexiglas didn't break or crack. I thought, *If I am to survive, I will need to use my hands and get this cuff off.* I felt confined and restrained. Desperate, I kept clawing to get the handcuffs off my left wrist. My skin was breaking beneath the metal of the cuff. *I have to escape.*

I stopped moving when I saw him come in from outside. He didn't even look at me as he went upstairs to the loft apartment. Almost trance-like, my body stilled. I retreated to the innermost safety of prayer:

> *God, act as a shield against any harm to myself and my family;*
> *Thank You, Father, that You have me in the palm of Your hands;*
> *God thank You that no weapon formed against myself or my family will prosper.*
> *Give me strength to get out of this car; God, please help me.*

I repeated this mantra over and over in my mind, then audibly to my own ears.

Miraculously, I finally ripped free of the cuffs. My left wrist bled from the fresh claw marks. I still have the scars as a lifelong reminder of my terror and survival.

Fight or flight. I did both.

I reached around the window divider on the passenger side, but the Plexiglas didn't budge. I tried the other side, and suddenly it gave way. By the grace of God, there was just enough of an opening for me to get through. I crawled in the front seat and opened the driver's side door. I ran for my life.

Knowing he was still up in the loft, I bolted straight for the woods to the right. There were no windows on that side so Gabriel wouldn't see me. I managed to get through our property line to where I saw a truck on a neighbour's property. I didn't want to involve anyone, so I went to the truck there. I checked the back door, and it was unlocked. I jumped in and quickly looked around for something warm to wear. The dome light came on and I freaked out that he'd see me. But within seconds, the light dimmed. I was freezing. As I reached around I felt nothing but tools. I saw a neon vest, but I definitely didn't want that. My heartbeat was racing beyond my breath. I couldn't stay here. *If he lit fire to all our vehicles, what if he did the same thing to this one?*

I jumped out and dashed for the woods. The spindly trees whipped about my face and head as I tried to move deeper into the forest. I was terrified that every branch cracking beneath my weight would give me away. I crawled on my hands and knees in order to get through them. The tie on my wrist trailed behind me and kept catching on twigs and branches. I pulled it off.

With no light but the moon, I kept moving in my bare feet, wincing in pain. Explosions like firecrackers filled the night air. My ears were hypersensitive to every unfamiliar sound. I dragged my body for what seemed like forever. I finally came upon a fallen tree trunk with big roots. *Thank you, God.* I crouched like an animal in its hollowed opening. I thought nothing of the dirt and leaves that must have been crawling with bugs. With great relief, I molded the cavity with my body as tightly as I could. The cold began biting at me. My body throbbed all over until numbness set in. Finally, feeling somewhat safe, I wept as I stared into the darkness.

I lost track of time. I stretched my black yoga pants over my frigid feet, tying a knot to cover them. I was afraid of frostbite. I could see my breath, so I tried to breathe beneath my thin top so its vapours couldn't be seen. The sounds baffled me. The bangs echoed loudly as if in a war zone out there. I kept wondering, *Where are the fire trucks? Where are the police? The ambulances? Doesn't anyone see what is happening?*

Through the woods, I saw another house on fire in the distance. Flames shot up high into the sky. Suddenly I heard two guys freaking out. *Maybe they could help me?* I didn't want to yell out in case Gabriel could hear me. I thought if I could get to them, I'd be safe. I felt around and picked up a stick to help prop myself up. I stepped forward using my makeshift cane, but it snapped beneath my weight. I fell to the ground. Then I heard whistling. *Oh my God. Is that Gabriel? Was he taunting me?*

"Hey boys." It sounded like Gabriel's voice.

Two shots rang out, startling me, followed by dead silence. *It was him*; *I knew it was*. Alarmed at how close Gabriel was to me, I crawled as fast as I could back into the hollow of the fallen tree. The woods fell silent again. As I peered out, I saw what seemed to be a shadow of a man holding a rifle. I couldn't tell if I was hallucinating or not. I froze with fear, praying to God again and again.

After some time, an opening through the trees revealed a black, tank-like truck with bright lights racing up and down the dirt road. I remained hidden. I heard another voice through a megaphone: I strained to hear if it was the Colchester Police, but they didn't repeat it. I thought maybe it was the police or, could it be Gabriel? He owned one of those microphones. Mentally exhausted, I thought he could be taunting me. I couldn't be sure. I decided to stay put until morning when I could see.

During the night I could see stars in the sky, and nocturnal sounds filled the woods. *Had I survived being killed by my partner only to be eaten by a bear?* I felt around for something to protect me. There was a rock—at least it was something and it seemed to calm my paranoia. All night I continued to pray for my family, who I would learn had experienced their own nightmare—along with our unsuspecting neighbours.

WHAT HAPPENED

Crime Scenes in the Portapique Community
Official Timeline and Victims

April 18 10:00 p.m.–10:45 p.m.[4]
10:00 p.m. (estimated)

The perpetrator arrived at the Blair residence on Orchard Beach Drive, 81 metres from the warehouse at approximately 10:00 p.m. The perpetrator shot **Greg Blair** on his deck while his wife, **Jamie Blair**, called 911 from inside saying there was a police car decked and labelled RCMP in the driveway. She identified the perpetrator by his first name. She hid with their two children in her bedroom. While talking to 911, the perpetrator shot her through the bedroom door. The two children, ages ten and eleven, remained hidden then fled next door to Lisa McCully's house when the perpetrator left. Before leaving, he shot the family pets.

10:05 p.m.–10:20 p.m. precise movements of the perpetrator are uncertain.

The Blair children ran to their neighbours, where Lisa's children let them in but **Lisa McCully**'s cellphone location data suggests that she had exited her residence and was on or near Orchard Beach Drive at 10:08 p.m. It appears plausible that the perpetrator encountered Lisa McCully at that time while driving south along Orchard Beach Drive toward Cobequid Court and shot and killed her.

After the perpetrator killed Ms. McCully, he travelled south in his replica RCMP cruiser to Cobequid Court to the residence of **Joy and Peter Bond** and the residence of **Jolene Oliver**, **Aaron Tuck**, and **Emily Tuck** (seventeen, the youngest victim) and fatally shot the five residents, all of whom were later found by police, located near the entrances of their respective homes.

10:20 p.m.–10:25 p.m. (estimated)

The perpetrator arrived at 71 Orchard Beach Drive, the residence of **Frank and Dawn Gulenchyn,** sometime before 10:25 p.m. He parked his vehicle in their U-shaped driveway, with his vehicle facing south and his driver-side door closest to the Gulenchyn's front door. He shot Frank and Dawn Gulenchyn and then set the home on fire.

10:27 p.m.–10:39 p.m. (estimated)

Sometime after 10:27 p.m. the perpetrator turned south on Portapique Beach Road. He then travelled past his cottage, which was ablaze, to the residence of retired couple **Joanne Thomas and John Zahl** at 293 Portapique Beach Road. The perpetrator shot them both before setting their home on fire.

Corrie Ellison, who was in Portapique with his brother Clinton, visiting their father, left his father's residence on Orchard Beach Drive on foot at roughly 10:30 p.m. and walked north to investigate the fire at the perpetrator's warehouse.

10:38 p.m. (estimated)

The perpetrator used a trail through the woods (the same trail he had dragged Lisa along earlier) to travel from the southern portion of Portapique Beach Road to the warehouse at 136 Orchard Beach Drive. He emerged from the driveway at approximately 10:40 p.m. and turned right onto Orchard Beach Drive, where he encountered Corrie Ellison and fatally shot him. Clinton discovered his brother's body and fled into the woods. Using his cell phone, he called 911 and was rescued at 2:30 a.m. when the Emergency Response Team called his name over a megaphone speaker.

10:40 p.m.–10:45 p.m. (estimated)

Perpetrator left Portapique via a 'blueberry field road' after killing thirteen people in the first hour

After encountering Corrie Ellison on Orchard Beach Drive, the perpetrator travelled south, to the intersection of Cobequid Court, then turned left and proceeded east on Cobequid Court to the blueberry field road. The perpetrator then turned left, and proceeded north on the blueberry field road, connecting to Brown Loop. From there, prior to or around 10:45 p.m., the perpetrator then accessed Hwy 2 via Brown Loop or Clark Road, managing to evade RCMP at the entry to Portapique Beach Road.

13

Rescued

SUNDAY, APRIL 19, 2020

While I laid shivering and numb inside the cavity of a tree, my family and other innocent neighbours were drawn into the chaos unfolding in Colchester County. Fear turned to panic throughout the night and into the morning as the RCMP scrambled to capture Canada's worst mass shooter in history.

After Gabriel left our cottage, he lit our warehouse and other homes on fire, shot, and killed people he liked and others he didn't even know. The thirteen hours of mayhem that had begun with me continued with every hour, as Gabriel moved across rural Nova Scotia in his replica RCMP car that looked so real that it fooled even the police.

MAUREEN:

AT 3:30 A.M., I awoke alarmed at the sound of pounding on my front door. My heart sank. A middle-of-the-night visitor or phone call could only mean one thing: something is wrong. I grabbed my housecoat and stumbled toward the stairs. I vibrated with impending dread that my twenty-one-year-old daughter Emma was in danger. As a single mom, I had experienced lots of heartache with Emma throughout her teenage life. Now that Emma lived on her own, I never stopped worrying about her.

When I saw the police, my knees buckled. I couldn't move, as my mind raced with thoughts of Emma injured or dead. Barely breathing, I opened the door to two officers from the Halifax Regional Police.

"Are you Maureen Banfield?"

"Yes," I managed. "Is Emma OK??"

"Who's Emma?"

"My daughter, Emma."

"Oh, Ms. Banfield, this isn't about your daughter. We are here about Lisa Banfield. You are her next-of-kin. Do you know where she is?"

My body responded to the relief it wasn't Emma, then to despair when I heard Lisa's name.

I always feared something awful would happen to Lisa. "Oh my God. Is she dead? Did he kill her?"

The officers tried to calm me and took me toward the living room to sit down. "That's why we are here. Do you know where your sister is?"

"Yes, she's with Gabriel. They are in Portapique at their cottage. It's their anniversary weekend. I spoke with her around 3 p.m.; they were out for a drive. What happened?" I sputtered words faster than my brain could process.

"There's been a shooting in that area."

Then I couldn't breathe or speak.

"We are liaising with the RCMP there trying to get as much information as we can. Right now, we have not located Mr. Wortman or your sister, Lisa."

They fired question after question at me, leaving me more scattered and afraid. They asked about the layout of the land in Portapique. I gave them a blueprint of the property I owned next to the warehouse.

They wanted all the addresses and telephone numbers of our siblings. They also asked about the guns Gabriel owned.

I knew he had some, but never saw them. I showed them pictures from my cellphone of Gabriel, including the one Lisa had taken at 6 p.m. that night, as well as the warehouse and cottage. The RCMP asked me to evacuate my home. As limited information filtered to the RCMP, I called Janice to come to the house so we could all be together as our entire family was being transported to RCMP headquarters in Burnside, Dartmouth.

I finally reached Janice, and she expressed the same sinking realization: *He finally hurt Lisa.* Janice took so long to arrive that I had an ominous fear that Janice had headed to the Dartmouth clinic to look for Lisa.

I called her back. "Where are you? You went to the clinic, didn't you? I told you to come straight here."

Janice sat in her car alone at the top of the steep driveway to our Dartmouth home. "I was just checking to see if she was home. There's no one here," she said cautiously.

In a split second, I heard terror screams from Janice, "Don't shoot, don't shoot!"

Sirens wailed and chaotic voices drowned out Janice's pleas. SWAT officers bellowed, "Get out of the car! Get out of the car! Show your hands! Get out! Get down!" The phone went dead.

Not knowing who she was, police in SWAT gear, with guns drawn, swarmed Janice and took her from her car.

* * *

I SURVIVED

6:28 a.m. Orchard Beach Drive, Portapique

At sunrise, I thanked God that I made it through the night. I started moving on my hands and knees from my burrow, but stopped suddenly. *What if he's still out there?* I turned back and laid there in silence for what seemed like a half hour or more trying to decide what to do. *I can't stay here all day; I need to get help.* I convinced myself to try. My cold, bare feet didn't even feel the pain from the uneven gravel. My body mindlessly moved toward safety. I prayed, *God, guide me out of here.*

When I reached the ditch that bordered the woods, I saw Leon Joudrey's grey house. I didn't know him well, but he had done a few jobs for Gabriel. His dog barked as I approached, and he let me in. I desperately scanned the room and bolted for the bathroom, thinking Gabriel is going to find me. I asked him to call 911. I was trembling when he handed me his cellphone, but I dropped it. Leon picked it up as my hands were shaking. "Hello," I could barely speak.

"Hi Lisa, we're going to help you OK, stay on the phone with me. You're not injured, are you?"

"I'm in pain now. My back."

"We're going to get you some help and then we're going to get you some medical attention."

Through the windows we could see uniformed SWAT teams coming up the driveway. Just hours earlier, RCMP investigators had assumed I was dead, burnt in the fire that destroyed our home.

Leon's dog barked again when an armoured truck let out a small army of police, who created a perimeter of protection in the yard. I still feared Gabriel would suddenly appear and shoot me. They took me to the end of Portapique Beach Road, then immediately transferred me into an awaiting black SUV. The RCMP had set up a coordination checkpoint near the Great Village Fire Hall. A member of the Emergency Medical Response Team did a quick examination and found me "moderately hypothermic," as my body wasn't circulating heat and my lips had a hue of blue. Constable Ben MacLeod would write in his notes that I was "fearful for my life" and in "a state of terror," with a distraught, disheveled appearance. He noted that he had only seen one other person in his career who was petrified to the same extent: a woman who had been kidnapped and held captive for three days.[5]

I had trouble walking because my lower back throbbed in ceaseless pain. They transferred me to an ambulance for initial treatment. The female attendee was immediately comforting and showed me such compassion. I had a momentary feeling of safety.

RCMP officers drove me to a checkpoint they'd set up in Great Village. They were asking questions but my thoughts were spinning acutely aware that Gabriel was still out there. Upon arriving, I was immediately placed into an awaiting ambulance where the paramedics covered me with blankets and pumped painkillers into me. Constable Terry Brown and Constable Dave Melanson asked me questions. I warned them about the white decommissioned police car Gabriel owned. I could tell they thought it was just a normal ghost car, so I emphatically repeated, "No, it looks exactly like your police cars . . . with stickers. It looks identical . . . the lights on the top." I told them about the guns he took with him in the front seat and how he handcuffed me. Then I told them about hiding in the woods.

They wanted a description. The last time I saw Gabriel he was clean-shaven, wearing black jeans.

I asked if my family was safe because Gabriel said he was going to Dartmouth to burn the clinic and then go to Maureen's.

Shortly before 8 a.m., I arrived at the Colchester East Hants Hospital in Truro and was examined again. My medical record noted I had tenderness in my lower right flank; superficial scratches and abrasions on my hands, feet, and legs; and bruising on my upper back and left wrist and hand. X-rays revealed fractures in my ribs and lumbar spine.

Neither hospital staff nor RCMP took pictures of my injuries. An officer was posted outside my room for protection.

No one told me innocent people had been murdered overnight. According to records, within hours of being admitted another constable asked me questions about the previous night.

I still feared for my family's safety. Gabriel was still out there. I would soon learn that my sisters and brothers had already been drawn into the RCMP investigation. The police gathered them in the station with supervising officers in a glassed-in conference room. The police still hadn't apprehended Gabriel and had no idea where he could be hiding out. They separated my family members for individual interviews in rooms wired for sound and video. Without exception, my family told them as many details as they could about Gabriel. Maureen gave the RCMP pictures that Sunday in the early hours—images that were later used in news conferences, including the BOLO (Be On the Look Out) picture of Gabriel Wortman (with my image edited out), his replica car with the fleet number, and pictures of other vehicles he owned.

Maureen also told the police about the large amount of money Gabriel had recently withdrawn and worried that may be part of what was unfolding—could it be a robbery gone bad? Hell's Angels? She helped them realize how many police cars Gabriel had collected, and that he owned an RCMP uniform. Janice recounted how I'd sent her the anniversary photo at 6 p.m. the night before, as she described Gabriel as a narcissist. She shared that her biggest fear was that Gabriel would kill me and then himself.

My family told the RCMP anything and everything they could remember to help them find Gabriel. They shared their own impressions and stories of Gabriel's psychotic behaviour, especially with me, his obsessive buying habits, and his fascination with guns. All of it was recorded as each freely provided their statements without regard for their own legal jeopardy.

Both my brother and brother-in-law independently told officers details about their relationship with Gabriel. They knew about his gun collection and how he'd use the mud flats of the basin for target practice. They shared that I had asked them to purchase some bullets from Canadian Tire for Gabriel because they were hunters. I wish I never asked my family to get them.

* * *

Unfortunately, because of COVID restrictions, I could have only one family member stay with me that Sunday evening. Maureen arrived at my hospital bed twelve hours after my rescue. She never left my side. I told her everything. We cried as relief washed over us.

Given my traumatized and medicated state, Maureen asked the hospital staff once again if Janice could come help. Under these extraordinary circumstances, they agreed. They brought in a cot so they could take turns looking after me. My "trauma brain" struggled to remember sequential details of what happened. I hardly slept, as my thoughts were consumed by so many unanswered questions. *What had Gabriel done? Why? Did he plan this? Where was he?*

WHAT HAPPENED

Crime Scenes Wentworth to Enfield
Official Timeline and the Other Victims[6]

Sunday, April 19, 2020
12:00 p.m.–1:00 a.m.(estimated)

Three community members, including two youths, provided statements to the RCMP that, after midnight, they had seen a police patrol cruiser in the Debert Business Park, 42 kilometres from Portapique. During their anniversary drive Saturday afternoon, Lisa and Gabriel had visited the former Canadian Forces site commonly known as the Diefenbunker.

5:42 a.m. (estimated)

The perpetrator appeared to have stayed in the Debert Business Park overnight. At approximately 5:42 a.m. a local bakery captured video of the replica RCMP cruiser travelling east on Ventura Drive out of the Debert Business Park. He was wearing parts of an RCMP uniform, including the pants and shirt.

6:35 a.m. (estimated)

Shortly after 6:35 a.m., the perpetrator travelled along Highway 4, avoiding the main Trans-Canada Highway and arrived at 2328 Hunter Road, the rural home of **Alanna Jenkins and Sean McLeod.** The perpetrator knew the couple, both of whom worked for the Correctional Service of Canada. He remained at their home for three hours. He shot one of the family dogs, then shot Alanna Jenkins and may have shot Sean McLeod before setting the house on fire.

8:50 a.m.–9:15 a.m. (estimated)

Tom Bagley left his home on foot for his usual morning walk along Hunter Road. During Mr. Bagley's walk, he passed the Jenkins/McLeod residence and would likely have observed smoke and fire. Prior to 9:20 a.m., Mr. Bagley went to the home, presumably seeking to assist or to ascertain whether assistance was needed. He was shot and killed by the perpetrator.

8:55 a.m. (estimated)

Kristen Beaton was a continuing care assistant employed by the Victorian Order of Nurses and was expecting a second child. Sometime before 9:00 a.m. Kristen posted on a Facebook group called "Local 35 Home Support Workers." The post contained a link to the RCMP Twitter page that was warning of an active shooter in Portapique who is armed and dangerous, and the message: "Anyone working in [District] 5 and 7 please be safe and keep your eyes open."

9:23 a.m. (estimated)

The perpetrator's replica RCMP cruiser was captured on video travelling south on Hunter Road toward Highway 4, approximately 3.7 kilometres south of the Jenkins/McLeod home. He was wearing a ball cap and now had on a reflective vest.

9:30 a.m. (estimated)

Lillian Campbell was on her daily walk along Highway 4 in the forested Wentworth Valley dressed in an orange visibility vest, unaware of the events in Portapique, when the perpetrator passed her. He slowed down the replica RCMP cruiser, turned the vehicle around and pulled up beside her, and shot her dead. He then proceeded south toward the northeastern town of Truro, an hour away from Halifax. There was no evidence he knew her.

9:59 a.m. (estimated)

Kristen Beaton was driving to Masstown and Debert to meet clients. It appears that shortly before 10:00 a.m., she parked her Honda CR-V on the gravel south side of Plains Road, Debert, to make some phone calls. The perpetrator was travelling on Plains Road when he slowed his vehicle, and drove his replica RCMP cruiser next to Kristen's CR-V. He then shot Kristen Beaton through her driver-side window. Throughout the morning, Kristen had exchanged multiple text messages with her husband, Nick Beaton, about the events involving the active shooter as they unfolded, but she did not know the perpetrator.

10:00 a.m. local (estimated)

Heather O'Brien was a licensed practical nurse also employed by VON, but she was not working that Sunday, rather she was driving to deliver her daughter a coffee. O'Brien passed the perpetrator and Kristen before pulling her Volkswagen Jetta over to the south shoulder of Plains Road approximately 260 metres from where Kristen's car was parked. She was on the phone with a friend when she said she saw a police cruiser. The perpetrator drove toward her and stopped his replica RCMP cruiser next to her car. He then got out of his vehicle and fatally shot Heather O'Brien through her driver-side window as her friend heard screams and gunshots over the phone.

At this point, the perpetrator had killed nineteen people.

Shortly after 10:00 a.m., Joey Webber left his residence to conduct a family errand. He was driving a grey 2008 Ford Escape SUV.

10:27 a.m. (estimated)

After gathering information about the previous night's events, local RCMP members took up various positions along the two-lane Highway 2. They were now looking for the perpetrator's Ford Taurus disguised as an RCMP vehicle. Constable Chad Morrison parked in Shubenacadie, roughly twenty minutes north of the Halifax Stanfield International Airport just north of the Shubenacadie River and south of the intersection of Gays River Road. **Acting Corporal Heidi Stevenson** and another officer parked on the median of the four-lane Trans-Canada Highway. She then headed towards Constable Morrison after a police broadcast says there is a sighting of the perpetrator.

10:40 a.m. (estimated)

Joey Webber arrived at the Esso Milford Wilson's gas station in Milford. He then drove north to the intersection known as the Shubenacadie cloverleaf because the roads interchange.

10:48 a.m. (estimated)

Constable Chad Morrison's vehicle was positioned north of Shubenacadie at an intersection that looks like a cloverleaf and the Shubenacadie River when he noticed a Ford Taurus police vehicle travelling south on Highway 2 toward him. While he thought this was Acting Corporal Stevenson, it turned out to be the perpetrator who pulled his vehicle up next to Constable Morrison. He pointed a handgun out of the driver-side window and fired at least three shots. Constable Morrison "hit the gas" and broadcasted that he'd been shot by the perpetrator. He confirmed that the perpetrator was driving a marked police vehicle.

10:49 a.m. (estimated)

As Acting Corporal Stevenson was driving up the cloverleaf ramp, the perpetrator, who had continued driving south on Highway 2 behind wounded Constable Morrison, entered the same intersection, turned his vehicle and travelled across the opposite lane and into the one-way ramp, toward Acting Corporal Heidi Stevenson's oncoming vehicle. He rammed her in a head-on collision and they came to a rest almost perpendicular to one another after the collision.

Acting Corporal Stevenson fired at the perpetrator as they exchanged gunfire. She exited her vehicle from the driver's door and was found on the ground. The perpetrator fired several shots toward her police car then shot her at close range where she lay, before taking her pistol and ammunition.

10:53 a.m. (estimated)

Good Samaritan Joey Webber saw the accident with the two RCMP cars and drove up the ramp and stopped close to the two vehicles. He got out and approached the perpetrator. It appeared that the perpetrator directed Webber to the back seat of the replica RCMP cruiser. The perpetrator shot Joey while in the backseat of the replica RCMP cruiser. The perpetrator then set fire to the replica cruiser and drove off in Joey's grey Ford Escape SUV south toward Milford.

10:58 a.m. (estimated)

Gina Goulet, a denturist living in a rural house along the highway Wortman was travelling, texted with her daughter that she had heard about the "active shooter in Portapique" on CBC News and she was scared because she knew the perpetrator. The perpetrator likely arrived at Gina's home around 10:58 a.m.—the time of her last outgoing phone call to her daughter. He entered her home, shot her dog and found her hiding in her bedroom ensuite before fatally shooting her. The perpetrator changed out of his police clothing. Outside of Gina's, he left a grey shirt with an RCMP insignia on the shoulders, a neon traffic vest, and a red gas canister partially filled with gasoline. The perpetrator also left Webber's SUV at Gina's residence. In the stolen SUV, the RCMP later discovered a Correctional Service Canada navy-blue jacket and blue-coloured trousers with a yellow stripe. The perpetrator then stole Gina's grey Mazda 3 vehicle and headed toward the Halifax/Dartmouth area.

11:16 a.m. (estimated)

The perpetrator needed gas, so pulled into the Elmsdale Petro Canada gas station 14 kilometres away. The perpetrator was unable to refuel at the gas pump at which he initially parked and moved his vehicle to another pump. He then left the station without having obtained fuel and travelled south to Enfield on Trans-Canada Highway 102.

11:24 a.m. (estimated)

Roughly 35 kilometres from Dartmouth, where the perpetrator owned a home and where Maureen lived, he parked the grey Mazda 3 at gas pump number five at the Enfield Irving Big Stop and remained inside the vehicle. Two RCMP members were parked in their unmarked white SUV at pump number six. All that separated them was the gas pump and canopy pillar. The constables had memorized the perpetrator's face from photos that had been issued. One of the constables yelled, "It's him." Wortman raised a gun just as the constable drew his handgun from its holster and pointed it toward the Mazda 3. The other constable drew his firearm. Seconds later they shot the perpetrator, but forensic evidence later revealed that Gabriel Wortman shot himself in the head.

14

Victim or Suspect?

1 P.M. MONDAY, APRIL 20, 2020

LESS THAN FORTY-EIGHT hours after I fled for my life, Staff Sergeant Greg Vardy walked into my private hospital room. Unassuming, he wasn't stern or formal in any way. Dressed in plain clothes, he was stocky and balding. He sat close to my bed and as I agreed to give him a statement, he turned on a tape recorder. I didn't know then that he was a "truth verification" expert with the RCMP, or that he had thirty years' experience assisting in criminal investigations to help determine the truthfulness of witnesses, suspects, and victims.

"Usually nobody has a problem hearing my voice. I tend to be a little louder," he said with a Newfoundland accent, as he tried to lighten the awkwardness of the moment. S/Sgt. Vardy spoke plainly, casually, and without an urgency he must have felt as Canadians were glued to the news of the inexplicable tragedy that began with Gabriel's violent assault on me. His assuredness put me at ease.

"So, Lisa, I want to um, speak to you about the incidents over the last couple of days in relation to your boyfriend Gabriel," he began.

"Common law," I corrected him.

"First of all, I want you to tell me everything about the eighteenth, leading into the night when things started to happen. What

I'm looking for you to do, Lisa, is take your time, OK? Every single detail is very, very important—even if you don't think it's important, it is, OK?"

I began. "Our nineteenth anniversary would have been Sunday, but I said let's celebrate it on Saturday cause my sisters we have our bingo Sunday, so he was good with that, and it was a nice day. I made him breakfast . . ." I continued to recount what I remembered that morning.

For almost a half hour I recalled every detail I could about what happened. The anniversary drive, the return to the cottage, and then the night. I told him how Angel had pissed me off. I knew I wasn't making sense, but S/Sgt. Vardy just let me talk.[7]

"I apologized to Gabriel but at that point he was in a rage, 'Oh, you have to ruin everything,' and was just yelling and being rude. [I said,] 'I don't need to hear this, I didn't do anything, but I don't deserve what you're dishing out now, so I'm leaving.' I went back to the house, and I went to bed and then minutes later, he came back and ripped the blankets off me, and he just went psycho. He pulled me by my hair out of the bed and then started kicking me and hitting me and had me down on the floor."

I was all over the place; my mind jumped from one disconnected thought to another. S/Sgt. Vardy didn't interrupt me once, he just listened to me jabber on: "I said, 'I'm done with this, prior to, like we were talking about, buying the property in between our house and our cottage to put another garage and you know, positive, good things and then he went from this to that. But he's always been like a 'Doctor Jekyll Mister Hyde,' he could be so sweet on one hand, when it was bad, it was really bad and when it was good, it was great. But there was no even keel ever. It's how our relationship was."

I shared such embarrassing and shameful things. But I was desperate to help in any way I could.

Then S/Sgt. Vardy asked about Sean and Angel, our friends in Houlton, Maine. "Tell me about the people, what you talked about that got him upset at one point. Don't leave anything out."

I answered: "Sean was telling him how much he loved us both. We started reminiscing and he was talking about the time last year that we shut down our practice for two weeks and drove down there and took care of him for two weeks and waited on him hand and foot in his house 'til he got better. He told us he didn't know where he would be without us. So after I hung up with Sean we FaceTimed with Angel who was hanging out with her friends, having drinks. Then we said it was our nineteen-year anniversary so I didn't want to stay on the phone because we were celebrating and I said next year we're doing this commitment ceremony and Gabriel had the phone so he went to the bathroom. That's when I could hear her saying, 'Don't do it. Don't do it.' And I'm thinking, are you kidding me? It really pissed me off. I said, 'I'm letting you go, Angel, bye,' and I hung up. And that's when I said, 'I'm done, I don't want to drink anymore,' and I left. That's when I turned around and I thought I'm more pissed off at her than him. So, I went back and apologized, and it just continued to get ugly."

S/Sgt. Vardy asked me to retell the events repeatedly. "Tell me about the cuffs. You talked about him putting cuffs on one arm."

"They should be in the cop car. Didn't you find them? I was in the back seat, and I had them on one wrist and that's why I have a swollen hand because I kept trying to rip it off my hand. And I got it off, I just threw them in the car, and I went through the window and just ran."

Next S/Sgt. Vardy focused on the arsenal Gabriel had accumulated. "Tell me everything about those guns, ammunition, just take your time, don't leave anything out."

I answered as best I could while trying to make sense of all his questions. I just wanted to know what was happening now.

Only now, looking back, did I realize, he thought I knew more than I did.

I didn't stop to think, I just kept talking: "It was like the military sniper kind of guns that you watch on Rambo. He would always say anything could happen. If people try to break in, 'I want to be protected.' And what's really weird is a couple of weeks ago he was talking crazy again but said, 'I didn't want to tell you cuz you'll look at me differently.' I said: 'Gabriel, I love you. But you're scaring me. And he's just like, 'I will tell you another time.' He'd always tell me, 'When I go out, I'm going out with a bang. It'll be in the news.' I would just be like. 'Don't talk so foolish, Gabriel.' I would just dismiss it. I knew he had *crazy* in him, but I never thought he was serious. He valued his life and yet he used to say he wasn't afraid to die either. I don't know, I think he just liked to get a reaction out of me."

S/Sgt. Vardy tried to refocus me: "Let's go back and talk about guns and ammunition and when he got them. This is not about Lisa, about getting anyone in trouble. This is about understanding how all this happened, when it started, that kind of stuff. So just take your time and don't leave anything out."

I continued on freely. "He got his handguns down in the States and he would bring them back in his truck and when he'd say, 'Oh I got this gun,' I would say, 'I am not going to the States if you're bringing back shit like that. Like, I don't want to have anything to do with guns. Like, Gabriel, why do you need that many guns? You don't need that many guns.' He'd said, 'I just wanted to be prepared, you know, anything could happen, Lisa.'"

S/Sgt. Vardy continued: "Tell me about your relationship. Um, just about, you know, the volatility. And you've told me some things, but everything you say is important. It's important for us to understand, uh, what's gone on because other people have said they've seen things. So tell me about that relationship, anything he's said that really now you're thinking, 'Oh my God, could be connected.'"

I thought about it for a second. "The first couple of years it was really good, and he was loving and generous . . . Well, he cheated on me multiple times and I always took him back. And then the first time he hit me, I thought, 'I'm done,' and that was up here at the cottage, 'cause I've never had anybody hit me before so I ran away, got out of the situation. . . .

"For a long time, I was on eggshells and I didn't know, it would be no rhyme nor reason for it, he would just lose it and I would just try to calm him down and it would be fine. I ended up getting back with him again and again. It was good for so many years and then I told him the last time if he ever did it again, that would be it. I won't go down that road anymore with him. I was done 'cause I said, 'The older I get, I'm not putting up with your shit. I don't deserve it.'

"He was very controlling in the fact that he wanted me all to himself. I'm close to my siblings; I talk to them every day, could see them every day. But he didn't like that because he wanted all my attention. He was like a little boy in some sense that needed that constant, you know, build-me-up kind of thing."

S/Sgt. Vardy wanted to know about the people who were close to Gabriel.

"Hmm, he was a loner . . . He'd say, 'Lisa, if something happened to me nobody would care.' I said, 'A lot of people would care.' He never let anybody in totally 'cause he never wanted to get hurt and that's how he always was. He goes, 'I don't trust anybody, Lisa. I trust you; you're the only person in my life.'"

After talking for two hours straight, I needed a break. S/Sgt. Vardy left the room. When he came back, he switched gears. He wanted to know about specific people in Portapique and how Gabriel knew them. "Tell me about the neighbours, about the people in the area that you knew, um, that you had relations."

"They were nice enough. I mean, he said if you ever need them, it's good to be neighbourly and I said yeah, that's fine. Gabriel knew more of the neighbours than me because I just wanted it to be us. There's Jill and her husband, he had a good relationship with them. We did a lot for them because they were older. Allan and Joanne at the end of the trailer with their son, Peter. Peter split wood for us that morning.

"Gabriel knew more people in Portapique because he was there more often. He helped some with his backhoe to plow them out during a storm, or make teeth for them. Others didn't like him as much."

S/Sgt. Vardy began asking about certain neighbours. "And, um, also up there were, um, the Blairs."

"Gabriel would know all those guys because when he got the property on the back road, it's a private road, so they had fees and they'd have meetings and stuff and I never ever went to those. He knew them all, I didn't. I mean, I would wave and be friendly, but I wouldn't, you know, go over to their house for coffee or anything like that."

"Okay, do you know who the Blairs are, who we're talking about when I say the Blairs? Had two little boys, uh, ten and twelve years old."

"No."

"Okay. Um, are you aware of any relationships he had with any of those people? Like, were there any negative relationships? Was there anything that you thought that he doesn't like those people or this person or anything like that?"

I tried so hard to remember the names of all the people S/Sgt. Vardy asked about. I couldn't understand why he was asking about them. Then, I clued in. I blurted out, "Did he hurt them?"

"That's what I'm wondering, what was the relationship between them?" He clarified.

I didn't know many of the names mentioned in that interview, but I learned of their names and the other innocent strangers Gabriel brutally murdered. I pray for their souls and peace for their families every night.

Maureen and Janice had shared some details of their deaths. I was horrified and wanted to reach out to their families right away, but my lawyer told me not to talk with anyone. I wish I had ignored him. Not being able to offer my personal sympathy at that time to the other victims is a regret I still carry.

At one point during the interview, S/Sgt. Vardy asked me about Gabriel's feelings toward the police. I said, "He never liked them yet when he was young, wanted to be one. His uncles were in the RCMP, now retired. He always felt like he was one step ahead of them all the time, but was fascinated with them at the same time, hence getting that many [decommissioned police] cars. I said, 'For what? Why, Gabriel?'"

I understand how Gabriel's fascination with police vehicles seemed odd to outsiders, and it prompted me to question him, even though he had collected so many different things during our years together. His latest binge was decommissioned police cars from government auctions. He decorated a Ford in 2019 to look like a replica RCMP vehicle, adding a push bar on the front. But it wasn't licensed to drive. He'd tell me they were nice to have for a party, with the lights on, as a collector's item. He said he ordered decals off the internet. "He was addicted to the internet for years and he had the means to do it. I can't tell you why he collected so many things," I told S/Sgt. Vardy. "'Why are you wasting your money on all this stuff you don't need?' I'd ask him.

"'I just like it,' he said."

As the three-hour interview wrapped up, S/Sgt. Vardy asked me point blank if I thought Gabriel had planned this all along, but I really had no idea if he had.

A few days prior to his rampage, he said he knew when he was going to die, but I never imagined this. "Well, nobody knows that," I said to him.

"I know when I'm going to die."

"In your opinion, was there ever a plan in play at any time, or do you feel like he was making a plan to do something like this?" S/Sgt. Vardy asked.

"No. No. But he always said that he would go out with a bang. It would be in the news, that's what he said. And I'm like, 'Don't talk so foolish.' I would just shut it down 'cause I wasn't entertaining what he was saying, if you know what I mean."

I had a question of my own for S/Sgt. Vardy. "Can you tell me who he killed?"

"Actually, what I'm gonna do is . . . I want you to do a list of questions that you want to find out about," he said, not answering my original question. Now he was the one not making sense. "Things are changing fluidly over the last day and a half, so, um, I'll definitely do that."

He asked me for access to my iCloud photos, and of course I consented to that. I offered all the passcodes I could remember. I co-operated with everything the RCMP asked of me.

He said he would follow up on questions I had.

"You guys said you had him in custody and then the next thing I heard was that he was dead," I asked wanting to know what happened.

"So, an officer killed him?" I asked.

"That's my understanding," S/Sgt. Vardy replied. "I know you asked who else was deceased, so I'm not allowed to release that right now."

"Were there kids killed?" I asked.

"I can't say that."

My heart broke at the thought, and wondered if I hadn't escaped from the car, would it have prevented any of those people from dying?

I started to cry, "I'm so sorry. Like, that's the last thing I, I just think if I would've stayed with him then maybe he wouldn't have been looking for me." I gulped in air, trying to calm myself.

S/Sgt. Vardy leaned in, "Can I give you some advice? I've been at this a long time, all right? And I feel for you now. But I can give you a promise. There's nothing that you could've done that night to change this. You can either spend the rest of your life thinking, *what could I have done to make this different* and you're going to be a miserable woman because there's nothing you could've done. You can think about this, you can run it through your brain over and over, but you have to understand that you couldn't change this."

APRIL 21, 2020

Maureen became my advocate and translator as I couldn't think beyond my own physical and emotional pain. When the RCMP wanted to interview me again, with the help of a friend, Maureen helped find a lawyer, James Lockyer, one of the best, who lived in Toronto and could help us navigate the unbelievable tragedy that was unfolding. She told Mr. Lockyer that S/Sgt. Vardy wished to interview me again. Lockyer and S/Sgt. Vardy spoke. Lockyer advised him that I wanted to give the police investigators all the help I could, and he encouraged me to do this. He expressed concern that I might be a subject or target of the investigation. S/Sgt. Vardy told Lockyer that I was a "victim" and "in no jeopardy," and if in the future there was thought of wrongdoing on my part, I would be given all my rights, and immediate access to counsel. S/Sgt. Vardy advised Lockyer, "We are looking at Wortman and his crimes; we aren't looking at her at all."

He had recorded the date, time, and details of his conversation. Lockyer cleared us to continue to help RCMP in any way we could.

APRIL 24, 2020, FIVE DAYS AFTER

After being treated for my fractured rib and vertebrae, I was discharged. In some ways, I was afraid to leave the safety of the hospital. I felt confused and in disbelief at what Gabriel had done: first he set fires, killed thirteen people, then the next day murdered nine more innocent people. His bloody path, many steps ahead of the authorities, left Nova Scotian citizens in shock and paranoid that they could be next.

Agonizing grief fell on our entire province. The lives and relatives of the twenty-two murdered victims wounded everyone. They were remembered the night I was discharged from the hospital during a virtual vigil that included a moving fiddle duet by Natalie MacMaster with a clip of the youngest victim, seventeen-year-old musician Emily Tuck. The convergence of pain and the world's outreach of grace, love, and support flooded over us like a blanket: Nova Scotia Strong unified us, despite the pandemic's isolation.

***

I felt so lost. I couldn't return to my clinic home. I stayed at Maureen's house and Janice moved in as well. Blessed to have my family, nonetheless I remained in a catatonic state, oblivious to everything around me. Horrific slices of memories and images flooded without summon. And yet, any semblance of my pre-life erased, burned to the ground, and clouded with penetrable shame. I could only get brief moments of sleep induced by medications I needed to survive. Though I was grateful to be alive and with my family, my life was stunningly, numbingly different.

I reverted to a child, needy of everything, and knowing nothing. I couldn't function without the lockstep, hand-over-hand, moment-by-moment direction of my sisters. I needed their help even going to the bathroom. Janice and Maureen had become pillars to whom I clung for basic survival. Not survival from the life I escaped, but for a future life I couldn't imagine.

Sad and shellshocked, I couldn't begin to navigate the chaos of my life. Had it not been for my family, especially my sisters, I don't know what I would have done or where I would be right now. Then I would think of Gabriel's other victims. At least I had a future. I was grateful but feeling guilty about whether I could have done more. That thought filled the shadows of my consciousness.

Janice shared timely Facebook messages that made me feel human. One was from a former schoolmate, Beaver Bank, Nova Scotia:

> *I hope I don't upset you by messaging you at this horrible time for your family. Our family have known the Banfield's for years. We've all gone to school together. We are all old stock.*
>
> *Firstly, I know I speak for all of us when I say I'm truly sorry you are going through this. I know your family unity and strength will get you through. My heart hurts for all of you. I am a survivor of domestic violence. It's something I have kept quiet. Because it's hard. People judge you. People question you. It's a very scary place to be.*
>
> *Lisa is a hero. She fought for her life. She fought for the lives of others. She fought until the end. Every single day was probably a fight for her just to manage an abusive relationship. She is in my prayers for healing, peace, and strength. You all are.*

APRIL 28, 2020, TEN DAYS AFTER

At 4 p.m., the RCMP held a press briefing at which Superintendent Darren Campbell provided an update on the investigation to the media. "Our job is now to determine the actions of the gunman on

April 18 and 19. Though the gunman will never stand trial, we still have a duty to complete this investigation by the same standards that we would if he was," he told the reporters. It was then that I was publicly referred to as a "critical witness."[8]

That same afternoon, I sat down at the Dartmouth police headquarters with Maureen beside me. S/Sgt. Vardy wanted to question me again. His tone was similar as he asked for my signed consent to release my medical records, which I willingly did.[9]

Before he began with the questions he told me: "I guarantee you one hundred percent you're going to remember more detail. We're not in a rush, OK?"

"Okay," I said.

"I want you to realize that I mean you're here because you want to be here," he started.

"Mmm."

"I want you to be comfortable here today, but like I said you're, you wanted to be here to assist their police, and give them information."

"Ah-hum, yes."

"Obviously it's very important and I want to thank you for that."

"You're welcome," I said.

For the first time since the police questioned me, Maureen was asked to wait in the other room. My interview was being video recorded, so he said if I needed her, she'd be just next door. Maureen didn't like it, but it seemed to be the protocol for giving a formal statement.

Sergeant Fraser Firth escorted Maureen into the tech room to watch the interview live as it was being taped.

For the next six-and-a-half hours I cooperated fully.

S/Sgt. Vardy shared some information about what had happened during the past week. He told me our Portapique properties were being secured and cleaned up for the public's safety.

"How much damage? What is left?" I asked him.

"Oh, there's nothing left. There's just the foundation; everything is gone. Only ashes."

"Did you get the money from under the deck I told you about?" I drew a sketch of where to find the $750,000, while I was in the hospital.

He wanted me to draw it again and describe the duffel bag. Thankfully, it did not burn and became a large portion of the estate the families and I would eventually claim.

S/Sgt. Vardy had more questions about what guns Gabriel had and where he got them. Gabriel collected many guns and ammunition before I knew him. He asked about the two handguns and the military rifle I had referenced in my previous statement.

"Where did Gabriel get them?"

"Gabriel got the military one from Maine at a gun show, and one of the other guns from his friend who lived there. I think he inherited the other handgun." Gabriel went to the States a lot without me. He told me that he brought the guns back when he travelled by himself. He said he would never put me in that kind of position. He knew I didn't like guns and didn't want anything to do with them.

S/Sgt. Vardy then wanted more details on the bullets. He wanted to know how my brother and brother-in-law came to buy ammunition for Gabriel. I explained again that Gabriel was getting more and more paranoid about COVID. He constantly watched Trump's rants about the world's destruction. That's when Gabriel told me to ask my brother and in-law to buy some bullets.

"Why do you need more bullets? You have tons of bullets already," I asked him.

Gabriel pushed as he always did, "Because it could be the end of the world, and I want to protect us if somebody tries to take what we have. People can get desperate."

I called my family to ask. Initially they refused, but when Gabriel wouldn't let up, I called them again and they said they would.

I was as forthcoming with the RCMP as I could be. I didn't understand why Gabriel wanted more ammunition but never thought he'd actually kill anyone.

S/Sgt. Vardy kept circling back to that: "Lisa, like I told you already, you know, you've been very good to deal with. Even in the past there's been a little hesitation; you didn't want to get people in trouble."

I didn't know where his line of questioning was going. We'd already talked for hours. He left the room and when he returned, something was off. I could feel it.

"Obviously you came in today, to speak to us and be open and honest. You don't have to talk to me anytime; you don't have to be here. I feel obligated to say that to you because I want to be fair to you, as not only a police officer but as a human being. I'm not going to make any promise to you today," he said. "I'm not going to threaten you in any way, if you don't tell me. That's not how we operate, right?"

All I kept saying was umm. *What is he getting at? I always co-operated with the police. I wanted to help them investigate how this horror happened.*

"Everything we talk about can be used as evidence, obviously, OK?"

"Ah-hum," I nodded.

"So basically, whatever you felt you had to say before, you don't have to repeat to me here today and you don't even have to talk to me if you don't want to. I leave that to every single person that I speak with, right? Whatever you do say can be used as evidence, I said that to you and that's what I want you to understand."

I wasn't sure what he was trying to say. His body language and tone were different. I asked him, "So do I need a lawyer?"

Maureen told me she jumped up from her chair in the adjoining room. "Yes, she needs a lawyer. Stop this. That's not right," she demanded. Sergeant Firth told Maureen that she couldn't intervene,

Banfield Clan before Maureen, Joan, me, and Janice were born (1964).

Left to right: Gilbert, Beulah, Charles, Jimmy, Brenda, Dougie, and Beverley.

Lisa's school portrait, Grade 4.

In our backyard with our dog Colie. Left to right: Janice, Joan, Maureen, and Lisa (1979).

Our cottage home at 200 Portapique Beach Road (2019).

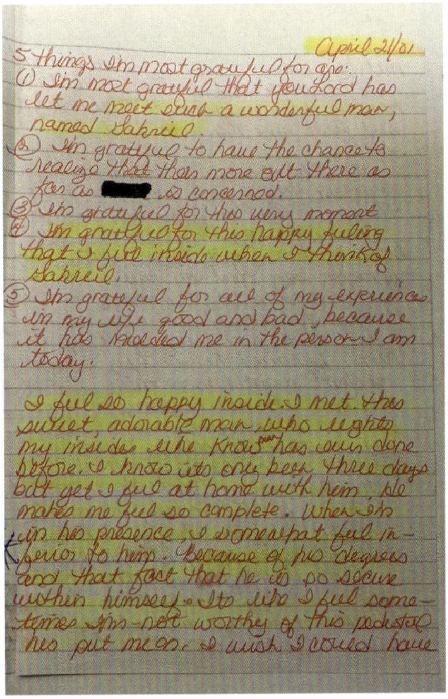

April 21/01

5 things Im most grateful for are:

(1) Im most grateful that you Lord has let me meet such a wonderful man, named Gabriel.

(2) Im grateful to have the chance to realize that theres more out there as far as [illegible] is concerned.

(3) Im grateful for this very moment

(4) Im grateful for this happy feeling that I feel inside when I think of Gabriel.

(5) Im grateful for all of my experiences in my life good and bad, because it has molded me in the person I am today.

I feel so happy inside. I met this sweet, adorable man, who lights my insides like know man has ever done before. I know its only been three days but yet I feel at home with him. He makes me feel so complete. When Im in his presence, I somewhat feel inferior to him. Because of his degrees and that fact that he is so secure within himself. Its like I feel sometimes Im not worthy of this pedestal hes put me on. I wish I could have

Actual diary entry (April 21, 2001).

Gabriel and I attending a family wedding (October 2019).

Our Portapique cottage remnants showing the burned vehicle, driveway, and entrance posts.

ANDREW VAUGHAN/THE CANADIAN PRESS

Atlantic Denture Clinic, Portland Street, Dartmouth, with infamous molded dentures decals.

SEAN DEWITT/WATERFRONT MEDIA HALIFAX

Sample of quilts made for our family from the Quilts for Nova Scotia artisans.

RCMP evidence identifying my sneakers worn that night in Portapique, taken from the MCC Inquiry.

The replica RCMP vehicle driven by Gabriel Wortman.

Maureen's cell phone picture of the tree that kept me safe that cold April night.

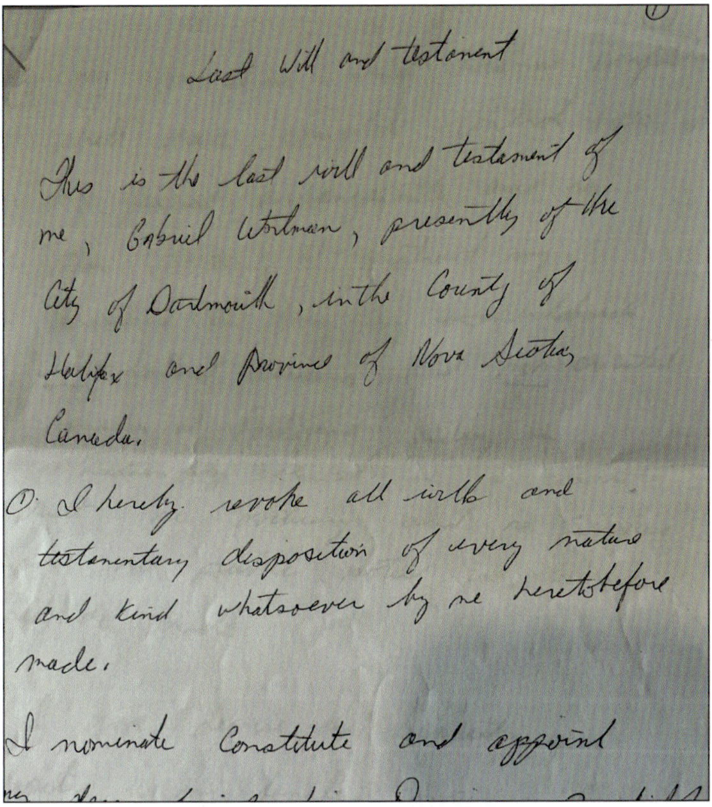

Last Will and testament

This is the last will and testament of me, Gabriel Wortman, presently of the City of Dartmouth, in the County of Halifax and Province of Nova Scotia, Canada.

(1) I hereby revoke all wills and testamentary disposition of every nature and kind whatsoever by me heretofore made.

I nominate Constitute and appoint

Gabriel's handwritten will.

The day of my testimony at the MCC Inquiry (July 15, 2022).

ANDREW VAUGHAN/THE CANADIAN PRESS

Me and my sisters (2023).

Me, Lisa Diana, present day.

and that only I could ask for a lawyer. Maureen was horrified at what this could mean for me. I was heavily medicated, and she felt I truly didn't understand what S/Sgt. Vardy was saying.

"Did she do anything wrong? Does she have anything to hide?" Firth asked Maureen.

"Absolutely not," Maureen retorted indignantly.

"Then she will be OK."

Maureen tried to settle herself as she watched me attempt to understand what was happening. Thankfully, she wrote copious notes on her phone, transcribing what was being asked so she could share it with my lawyer, James Lockyer.

When I asked S/Sgt. Vardy, if I needed a lawyer, Maureen's notes and the transcription of the recording reads: "No," then continued to confuse me with a kind of doubletalk.

"I'm saying to you that these are your rights." I was confused, but felt better when he said I didn't need legal counsel. S/Sgt. Vardy made me feel protected, and I trusted him. What we didn't realize until much later was that the RCMP weren't just asking questions to find out how and why Gabriel did this; they were laying the foundation for me to become the scapegoat.

15

Survival in My New World

THE DEVASTATING AFTERMATH of April 18 and 19, 2020, began with ashes. Nothing remained of my life in Portapique, except a bayside deck and two stone pillars identifying the address at the edge of our driveway. My thoughts were clouded by my stark, new reality. I faced being homeless, unable to work or sleep, and no hope for viable income.

Moving into Maureen's home was a blur. My sisters set up everything for me to feel safe. Maureen graciously gave me her master bedroom so I would have extra space, lots of light, and could lock my bedroom door. It was all I could manage just to say thank you, and then collapse. Acclimatizing to her place was challenging. Unfamiliar noises startled me and triggered my acute anxiety: the phone ringing, a car backfiring, the clanging of a pot, or—most alarming—a knock at the front door. My entire body was hypersensitive. I could feel my ears pulse as I strained to hear everything in my new environment. I was a wreck.

It was also weird living in Maureen's house when the home I lived in with Gabriel was only minutes away in downtown Dartmouth. Moving back above our denturist business wasn't an option. The sale of this property provided significant equity, adding to the overall estate. Losing everything in the fire, my sisters thought it would bring me comfort to get a few familiar things from my home. Adrienne Bowers, who was named trustee, sanctioned them to collect my clothing and any personal items.

For my sisters' safety, the Halifax Regional Police accompanied them. Yellow police tape still surrounded the two-storey building. A huge, plaster mold of smiling teeth accented the corner of our clinic home. They became a menacing symbol and reminder of the darkest days of 2020. There were cries to tear it down. In the months it took to sell, the building was vandalized and sprayed with graffiti. In January 2022, the new owners demolished what was our home for nineteen years.

Having a few of my familiar things gave me some comfort. Still, I felt like neither my life, nor my body, belonged to me. Besides my mental health, my broken ribs and lower back took the longest to heal and hurt every time I moved. The girls had to help me with everyday hygiene needs as I struggled with range of motion. My hands constantly throbbed and I winced with any pressure I placed on them. Looking at my bruises and the fresh scars constantly reminded me of my last beating from Gabriel and all he had done after my escape. I had been put on heavy drugs from my injuries and long-term medications to help manage the symptoms of post-traumatic stress disorder (PTSD) I was experiencing. Once again, I felt alone and tormented by my thoughts and petrified as to what was coming next.

The night terrors and nightmares were unrelenting. I was up all hours of the night: not wanting to sleep and not wanting to stay awake—always trying to feel safe. Gabriel was a vivid presence in my dreams every night. I remember screaming, yet no sound would come out—then I'd wake lathered in sweat. He'd always find me. I felt like I was reliving the reality I wanted to forget. Nothing stopped the flashbacks and horrifying thoughts of him hunting me and my family. If I got frightened in the middle of the night, not wanting to disturb Janice and Maureen, I would turn on all the lights until dawn broke through my curtains. They had nightmares, too. In the morning, we rehashed them as a way of releasing Gabriel's evilness from our collective minds. But this pattern lingered for months. To this day, he still *visits* all of us.

I became nocturnal, living in a stupor during daytime hours. I hated taking any medication, but for the first time in my life I needed to take drugs just to be able to function. I also struggled to eat. Just a month after the massacre, I wanted to stop taking the meds. I became so depressed that I couldn't get out of bed. I was losing feeling in my body. I felt like my organs were shutting down. Maureen called 911.

Arriving at the Dartmouth General Hospital, the emergency staff guarded me and treated me with great care. They sedated me and gave me several bags of intravenous fluids and painkillers. I was exhausted and dehydrated. Once I was released, the hospital arranged for a nurse to come to the house to administer medication if needed. It took a few weeks before the medication stabilized, and I could finally sleep at night.

Ironically, the isolation restrictions of COVID helped me feel safer when I went out in public. Even when they were lifted, I wore a mask if I had to go anywhere, so I wouldn't be recognized. Media vans had found our house; so too could anyone wanting to hurt me for what Gabriel had done. Every time I ventured out, I remained on high alert.

When strangers recognized me, I didn't know if they were haters. I was always startled when any stranger called out, "Lisa? Are you Lisa Banfield?" Until I understood their intention, I froze. Then their humanity calmed my trepidation: "I'm so sorry. I just want you to know how incredible you are; how brave you are." In fact, none of the strangers I met were ever hostile toward me. Instead, they were very kind and supportive. Some women shared that they had experienced violence in relationships, too. We immediately felt a bond and, despite the threat of the virus, instinctively embraced each other. Those gestures reminded me that I was not alone. Their warmth touched me at a time when I felt so scared and lost. I am profoundly grateful for those who showed me compassion.

I slowly gained strength by walking daily with my sisters in our neighbourhood. I went from only walking a block with both sisters assisting me on either side, to longer walks within my subdivision. I craved our daily routine. We met other walkers who greeted me with genuine kindness. I remember one morning when I was out with Janice.

A lady yelled from across the street, "You!"

I stopped in my tracks.

"You!" she pointed.

I felt afraid when I realized she recognized me. Friend or foe? Then I met her eyes.

She smiled at me as she clasped her hands in a prayer motion pointed to the sky, "You go, girl. God's got you!"

My shoulders instantly relaxed in relief.

"Thank you." Janice and I responded in unison; our eyes filled with tears. Her energy and spirit immediately lifted us.

Gradually, I started living my new life; I wanted some autonomy. I needed to replace my cellphone Gabriel destroyed that night. Because for me, if something happened, I knew this time I could get help. It made me feel safer. I took short drives to a community lake, where I would sit for hours soaking up the sun and writing in my journal. It is here that I would reflect on my weekly therapy sessions and attempt to find peace. Between my spiritual readings and my music, I was able to calm my thoughts and build on the possibility of hope. I gained a sense of freedom as I grew more comfortable in my new community.

"Skipper," the RCMP liaison officer, gave updates to the families of the victims and me. He conveyed positive messages of support from the public. One beautiful summer morning in 2020, Constable Wayne "Skipper" Bent came to the house with a special delivery. Caring Canadians had come together to form Quilts for Nova Scotia; this group of artisans spanned Newfoundland to British Columbia. They crafted personalized quilts for each of the twenty-two victims as well as for the unborn child. Each of their family members was also gifted quilts. The story they told through each unique panel was incredibly meaningful. Every quilter personalized theirs with a unique message: "NS Hugs, we hold you in our hearts," "NS Strong," or "Hope Lives." That tangible show of love gave each of us such comfort in those initial months.

People around the world were saddened by the tragic events that deeply affected the rural communities of not just Portapique, but Wentworth, Debert, Shubenacadie, Truro and Milford as well. Throughout our province, NS Strong decals hung in neighbourhood windows and vehicles. Amid the anguish, our whole province became unified, expressing love for each other. Generous donations poured in from people across Canada and beyond. The Red Cross collected $6.2 million for the victims of the Nova Scotia mass shooting. The Stronger Together Nova Scotia Fund contacted victims' families and all others impacted by the tragedy. They initially provided financial relief for my immediate daily needs, and I was grateful for the support.[10]

JOURNAL ENTRY: MAY 17, 2020, ONE MONTH AFTER

I so struggle with my feelings toward Gabriel. I truly loved this man, but yet I feared him at times. How do I see that as love? I could never imagine my life to have changed so drastically out of one horrific night! I would never have believed that he could be so heartless and cold! I really don't want to believe that he would have killed me in the end and yet, I'm sure

> *he would never have let me go either. I truly never would have thought what should have been a special day would go so bad. I didn't see that coming—at all! In the past when he was physical with me, I could sense it coming, just by his presence and the way he would react to certain things. But not that night. We were planning our future together.*
>
> *I'm thinking about my life now and it's like I'm looking at it from the outside in. While I still feel lost and alone, yet far from being alone because I have the greatest gift anyone could ever ask for, that's my family.*

I was so blessed and so fortunate; sadly, so many others were not. My journals revealed the ugly truth; I was living with a monster.

> *I wish I felt more like myself, so I could start to work on truly healing from the inside out. But the truth is, I'm different. I will never be the same, and perhaps that is a good thing. I will get there, I know I am strong and have the will to survive. I am truly so grateful to be alive and not to be afraid of Gabriel anymore.*

* * *

Shame's counterbalance is grace. And the grace of others sustained me through my daily existence. As much as I hid under the covers, people found a way to reach out. Neither Maureen nor I engaged in online social media, so Janice sifted through the anger and hatred people directed at me. The speculations, lies, and conspiracy theories, together with bitter criticism, were unrelenting. Janice would decipher which articles were valid in terms of facts and share them with us. The ones that falsely condemned me she'd only share with Maureen, especially those interviews, news features, articles, and podcasts that speculated about my supposed involvement. Leon Joudrey, the man who let me into his home that morning, told a reporter I didn't look like I'd survived a night in the woods—yet when you read the transcript of him during the 911 call, he described me and my state very differently.

Janice responded to messages on our behalf. All the positive posts and letters lifted my soul and truly restored my hope. Many women thoughtfully and lovingly shared their experiences of surviving domestic abuse; it was so inspiring and gave me a sense of humanity I needed in the darkest days of scrutiny. While words of encouragement from close friends and family buoyed all of us, it was the unexpected communication from strangers that ignited a fight in me I thought I lost:

> *Yes, I'm a complete stranger—and I will not write again as it's not respecting privacy—I just have a message I so wish her to know:*
>
> *I am a woman from Ontario who almost put my head through the ceiling jumping with joy when I heard she was alive! She survived!! That almost never happens—she is SO meant to be here!! I can't imagine what you all must be going through. I hope she feels safe. I need her to know she is not only a survivor but a true hero!!!*
>
> *HE killed those people.*
>
> *SHE saved countless lives and most importantly her own! His rage problem is NOT because of her! It's HIS problem—and he showed his evil toward everyone at last and she showed determination, courage, integrity, and how capable she is to push forward!!!! I hope she has more strength in the coming months, and if she doesn't she needs to remember Canada knows she's meant for this life and to live it the best she can with the people that matter most! Sending all my love and thankfulness to her and your family from me, a mother of three girls in Ontario ♥ My girls will know of her heroic actions when they are of appropriate age—and hopefully by then she will have a bright smile on her face that shows that no man can take no matter how hard they may try. We are proud of her*

and send her oodles of love and hope and will happily support GoFundMe for her. Remember: chapters end (even shitty ones) but this just means a new chapter awaits her! In private or in public form I just hope with time she heals and releases herself to allow for laughter and light and hope and love, because she deserves it ♥ God bless you guys xo and thank you for helping more people than you know.

PART IV

ON TRIAL

My life is still defined by a night that
will forever impact my future.

16

Returning to Hell

OCTOBER 2020, FIVE MONTHS AFTER

I WAS DETERMINED to return to Portapique before the snow fell. Anyone who suffers from PTSD will understand why returning to the scene would trigger and heighten the flashbacks, nightmares, and panic attacks I experienced that summer. I knew it would be grueling and awful, but I felt I needed to go. Janice and Maureen questioned if I was ready, concerned it would be too much for me. My clinical therapist warned it was risky for my mental health. Despite their cautions, I desperately wanted to find proof of my experience.

I remember S/Sgt. Vardy told me he had experience helping victims get closure this way and would join me. By now, the RCMP were facing intense scrutiny from the families of Gabriel's twenty-two victims and unborn child, who demanded an inquiry into the mishandling of the search for Gabriel during his rampage and failure to notify people sooner that he was posing as an RCMP officer. While my sisters paid close attention to the storm swirling around the police force's actions on that April weekend, I avoided the news. In my state, stories of despair of the families distressed me as I felt such deep sympathy and pain for all they were going through. Survivor's guilt haunted me. Federal Public Safety Minister Bill Blair finally announced the decision to hold a joint public inquiry with the provincial government. I did not have a clue what it would mean for me.

By now, I had given the RCMP complete access to my cellphone, which contained thousands of photos of Gabriel, his cars, and emails, exposing the intimate details of our life. I told them about the cash buried under the deck of the cottage. I drew them maps and told them where my coat might be along the ditch where I ran from Gabriel. I prayed to God we would find my jacket, the tie from my wrist, the tree hollow where I hid, and the rock that I held for protection during the night. They already found my necklace (I didn't even realize it was missing) and sneakers, but there were growing accusations and false stories that I was an accomplice and that I didn't escape and hide in the woods that night. I had to find that tree; I had to find my puffy jacket; I needed to *show* them the truth. I know what I lived through, what I survived. We called S/Sgt. Vardy, who set the date.

On October 23, 2020, I returned to Portapique for the first and last time since April 19, 2020. It was a crisp, clear, cool morning. Maureen and Janice drove me. We barely spoke during the ninety-minute ride from Dartmouth. I stared through the window at the infamous places on the highway route where Gabriel had shot and killed innocent people. I flinched as we drove by the Big Irving truck stop in Enfield, where he died. I struggled to keep it together as we passed the Shubenacadie intersection where Constable Heidi Stevenson bravely tried to stop him after he rammed her car head-on. She and bystander Joey Webber were among his last victims. Gabriel shot Constable Chad Morrison, who mistakenly took the replica car for his colleague Heidi's. He managed to drive away and survived his injury. Gina Goulet, a denturist Gabriel knew, was the last victim, murdered in her Shubenacadie home along with her beloved dog. It was chilling to think about where he'd been and what he did mile after mile unstopped. Even scarier to know that we'd been to some of the places he returned to that we had visited on the Saturday.

We had agreed to first meet at Masstown Market, a fifty-year-old fruit stand with fresh produce and baked goods, before heading to Portapique. I naively thought S/Sgt. Vardy was there to help me cope with revisiting the site. But I felt like he ambushed me. He pulled in next to us, and then another van with a team of people—including a videographer and Corporal Gerry Rose-Berthiaume—parked on the other side of us. I was visibly shaken. I didn't know any of them except S/Sgt. Vardy. They introduced themselves and said that they were there to capture the experience in hopes of learning anything new.

"Who is this for? Will this be made public?" Maureen asked directly.

S/Sgt. Vardy said he couldn't promise that, but made me feel like he'd protect me.

"We think it will help to find out more about how this happened," he said.

Maureen noticed my reaction and almost called it off. "With all due respect, I don't care what you need. This is about Lisa and her mental health." Maureen turned to me, "Lisa, you're shaking. Are you sure you still want to do this?"

We had come all this way and the thought of coming back at another time was more than I could bear. Besides, they were all standing there waiting for me. "Yeah," I said meekly.

We got into our separate vehicles and made our way to the entrance to our warehouse. Driving by the burnt homes of neighbours, now vacant lots where they had been murdered, sickened me. I was shocked at what I was seeing. My imagination spun and flashbacks of that awful night flooded my brain. Perhaps I wasn't ready?

The gate to the warehouse driveway was closed and locked, so we walked around it. No one else was there. It was an eerily quiet fall day. We stood in front of what used to be our large warehouse, now only a vacant lot with rocks and the remnants of an industrial-sized foundation. They asked that I begin where the argument took place on our anniversary evening.

A woman put some kind of mic-pack on me while a man held the video camera on us. They wouldn't let my sisters near me for support and told them to stay outside of the camera's view. I didn't know it at the time, but my heart-wrenching reenactment would eventually be posted for the entire world to see.

They pressed record; I looked into the camera and said my name.[11]

Cpl. Rose-Berthiaume stated the time and noted that my sisters and S/Sgt. Vardy, the polygrapher, were also present. "This is a reenactment today. I want to get as much detail as possible. You said it started here at the warehouse."

"Don't leave anything out" had become their mantra. I now realize they were truth-checking my statement. We stood under blue, sunny skies walking on the gravel yard near the empty, flattened slab of concrete of our warehouse. I pointed to where Gabriel had cleaned the Jeep and where all our other vehicles were parked that night. I showed him the trail I took through the woods to our cottage after Angel's hurtful comments and Gabriel's reaction.

We talked as we walked through the woods. I don't remember what I said until we emerged and I saw our property with nothing but the driveway signposts. Our cottage was gone; nothing but the unobstructed view of the Bay of Fundy remained. I bawled. Everything just hit me. The place I helped grow into a home, now levelled. I stared at the leaves on the ground where our house once stood. I felt inconsolable and failed to compose myself.

"I need a minute," my voice cracked in distress. I gasped. I couldn't believe it was all gone. I couldn't stop crying. "Sorry," I kept saying. I had to stop several times just to catch my breath. I felt like I was out of my body. It had been six months, and I crumbled.

"Take your time, Lisa, you're doing awesome," Cpl. Rose-Berthiaume said.

I just wanted to run. I couldn't focus on what he was asking. I wanted to wail and scream. I wished I had time to just be there, by myself, feel my grief, feel the loss of it all. Once again, I had to set aside my needs for others; they were all there waiting for me, taping me. I had to get it together. All the while, my sisters weren't able to console me.

As I told S/Sgt. Vardy the day after I was rescued, I repeated all I remembered about being beaten and dragged through the cottage before he lit it on fire. Then his threats for burning down the warehouse and the clinic in Dartmouth. In those moments, every emotion was relived. I felt dizzy, recalling my terror that night.

Emerging from the path, Cpl. Rose-Berthiaume asked, "Where do you go when you get back here?"

"Gabriel took me over here," gesturing to the entrance of where our warehouse used to be. I told them what Gabriel did next with jerry cans of gasoline: "I'm watching him as he is telling me not to move. First he threw it on his tractor and his truck that was parked by it, then doused all the other vehicles parked in the yard."

"We went into the warehouse and he had it locked up like we always did at the end of the night. If he planned on doing this, why would he lock everything up and clean his Jeep? He unbolted the warehouse and, in my mind, I'm thinking, *what if I just turn around and run*, but he was so close to me I wouldn't have a chance to get out of his grasp with whatever he had attached to me.

"Inside, he went over to where he kept the handcuffs by the bar. He put them on my left hand, and he said, 'Give me your other hand.' At this point I was close to the bar, and I said, 'Gabriel, it doesn't have to be like this.' That's when he told me we were going to the clinic then to Maureen's. I thought, *If you are going to kill me, just do it*, so I bent to my knees and covered my face."

The corporal told me to take my time. I grabbed his arm to show him how Gabriel grabbed me and threw me into the back seat of the car. Gabriel then went to the bar and got guns and more bullets before he returned and threw them on the front seat of the replica police car.

Going through this process was disturbing. Having to repeatedly retell the worst day of my life seemed revictimizing but they wanted me to tell it again, this time on camera. I obliged. It's an ongoing nightmare I cannot forget.

"I remembered getting out of the police car and how I opened the door and all I was thinking was, *just run*." I became distraught; fretting, once again about the what-ifs: "Why I didn't . . . Think about what I could have done."

The corporal tried to calm me. "You were trying to survive," he said empathetically.

I retraced my movements toward a small cottage beside ours. There was a thin bank of trees between our properties, then a shallow ditch. I led Cpl. Rose-Berthiaume across the road, trying to find the place where I noticed a truck. It looked different because of the seasonal change and so many of the familiar buildings were gone, burned down. He seemed to be leading me in a direction in front of a house. I know I didn't go this way. I became frustrated. I followed him anyway. When we got to the building, I told him again, I wasn't here.

I walked back to where we started. I remembered feeling something soft beneath my feet that night, so I looked for a spot on the property that seemed familiar. I continued to describe seeing a truck: "I saw a light on in a house, but Gabriel was after me. I didn't want to get anyone else involved so I headed directly to the truck. It was cold, so I jumped in the backseat of the truck. I felt around for something warm but there were only tools and a worker's neon vest."

I was disoriented that night and felt just as confused now trying to picture where I was at that moment. We returned to the road, and I tried to find where I had entered the deep woods. Cpl. Rose-Berthiaume asked my sisters to stay with S/Sgt. Vardy while he and the film crew followed me into the woods. Maureen ignored him and came anyway. I was so grateful, as I needed support reliving this.

As we headed deep into the woods the sun shone through the forest of fir trees and hardwoods. Moss, twigs, and fallen branches covered the ground. Because of the density of so many thin trees, the film crew were having technical troubles with the sound. At one point, my battery pack went dead, and they had to replace it. I could tell the corporal was getting frustrated. "We've been in these woods a long time. Are you sure you came this far?" I became exasperated, too. I had no idea how far I had crawled that night, but I wasn't leaving until we found it.

"Oh my gosh, it was a huge tree that was down with a hole that I buried my body in," I said, looking and looking deeper into the forest. "If I can just find that tree—sorry for taking you through all of this," I told him. I was praying to God, *please help me find it; I need to find it.*

"I think we should turn back. It's really hard to move through. It's OK, Lisa," Cpl. Rose-Berthiaume said as he started turning back.

This was my only chance to show them proof of what happened that night. Even Leon, our neighbour who helped me, had fuelled the conspiracy theorists by doubting whether I had hidden in the woods. I looked to my left and pointed to an overturned trunk, "This is it. Right here." I walked around to its opening. "And the rock, it's here. Yes, this is the rock." I was exhausted yet elated. The videographer kept taping while I saw Maureen taking her own pictures.

"This is where I heard the whistling and I remember seeing a fire over here"—I pointed in the distance—"and hearing the two guys and I probably got as far as here and dropped to my knees when I heard, 'Hey boys,' then bang, bang."

"What made you come out eventually?" Cpl. Rose-Berthiaume asked.

"I was just praying to God if I could make it to the morning, I could find my bearings in the daylight and get help."

I felt a huge wash of relief as we emerged from the woods. Maureen and I looked at each other. I did it. I found the tree and the rock.

We made our way back to the road. I found Leon's house where I took refuge that morning. At one point, a car approached, so I hid behind the corporal in case the driver recognized my face. Hiding had become part of my new life.

We stood down the driveway, looking at Leon's house.

"Is there anything we haven't talked about, or you haven't told us about that night?" he asked.

"I don't remember anything new," I said, staring at Leon's.

"You did a great job here today," he said. "Reach out to Greg or I when the stress goes down if you remember anything else."

They took off my microphone and drove off.

* * *

Finally, my sisters and I were alone.

Within minutes, S/Sgt. Vardy called us to say that a news vehicle was at the end of the road. This was shocking to all of us, as we had been in the area for a couple of hours without anyone around. It was only until the RCMP finished their filming did the media show up.

We decided to walk through the woods back to the seaside deck of our cottage, to avoid being seen. I knew this would be the last time to say goodbye to my life in Portapique. My therapist suggested I write Gabriel a letter and say everything I needed to for closure.

Maureen brought sage and wanted to have a brief smudging ceremony. She lit it, blew out the flame, and fanned its essence into the air and around each of us. We prayed for peace, purity, and the promise of healing for everyone hurt by Gabriel's actions. We hugged, cried, and exhaled in unison. I asked Maureen and Janice to leave me for a moment so I could say goodbye in private. They walked to the bottom of our rock wall beneath the bayside deck as I sat on the steps by myself.

Overlooking the low tide beach, I prepared myself to read my letter to him.

As I prayed, I heard this weird noise. I looked up to see an object hovering over my head. I can still hear the buzzing sound in my head. I screamed to my sisters.

"It's a drone," I yelled. Janice got to me first.

Maureen scaled the rock wall. It followed us. We ran past the cottage ruins, across the road and into the woods. We could hear it still above us as we huddled together under the cover of trees. I felt threatened, scared, and equally angry at the same time. How could this be happening? My private moment of healing was stolen.

I had no idea how awful it was going to get for me and my family.

* * *

It took months for the autopsy report to be released to me. As documented, Gabriel shot himself in the head within minutes of two officers firing on him. By mere and blessed coincidence, the RCMP officers were gassing up at Enfield's Irving Big Stop and noticed him at another pump. They surrounded him and shot him multiple times. This took place 35 kilometres from Maureen's house. The fact that this mass murderer's capture was a fluke is incomprehensible. To this day, I cannot fathom why, during this manhunt, a blockade was not set up on all the series highways and why the public wasn't explicitly warned.

There was no funeral. Gabriel always told me that he wanted his body to be buried in a Hudson's Bay wool blanket in the Portapique Cemetery, adjacent to our cottage. He had bought his plot soon after we renovated our cottage. In the end, after murdering so many innocent people, I could never honour his wishes. Instead, he was cremated and would never return to Portapique again.

"I don't want an obituary," he told me several times. He also didn't want his parents to know if anything should ever happen to him. But I thought, as a parent, I would want closure. After taking some remains for myself, I sent his boxed ashes to his parents in New Brunswick with a letter asking them never to contact me.

17

Scapegoat

DECEMBER 4, 2020, EIGHT MONTHS LATER

IN THE EARLY morning on a cold December day, my cellphone rang, displaying an RCMP number. Never a good thing, but as always, I answered. Cpl. Rose-Berthiaume, the same officer who took me through the reenactment, wanted to see me. There was an urgency in his voice that caught me off guard.

I was still in my bed, not even dressed, so I discouraged him. "Maureen's not here," I told him.

"That's OK. I only need to see you. I have to drop off some paperwork. It won't take long."

I called Maureen right away to tell her they would be at the house within twenty minutes. She had just left so she turned her car around and came back to the house.

Cpl. Rose-Berthiaume and another RCMP officer rang the bell. Maureen invited them to the living room where Janice and I sat on the couch bewildered, not knowing what they could want now. He handed me a sheet of paper, "I'm sorry to do this, but I have to serve you."

"What? What do you mean?" All I saw was the word "criminal." My heart stopped.

Maureen took the paper, asking, "What is happening?"

"We are charging you, your brother, and brother-in-law under Section 101 of the Criminal Code for the transfer of ammunition. We have to serve everyone this morning, as the news release will be made [public] by noon. We are sorry."

My first thought was, *Oh my God, am I going to jail?*

"Do I need to call my lawyer?" I blurted.

"I would, if I were you," he said matter-of-factly.

Janice and I burst into tears on the couch as Maureen was scrutinizing the paperwork. "Why now?" Janice asked. "From day one, we told you everything, including buying bullets. None of us had any idea what he was doing." My head spun. I was stunned and confused as to why the RCMP felt they had to penalize us.

The RCMP's press release became a compounded trauma that had consequential effects to this day:[12]

> *The tragic incidents spurred an investigation titled Operation H-Strong. Investigative teams were dedicated and worked tirelessly on this investigation to provide answers for the victims, their family members and the public. Though the gunman is ultimately responsible for his actions, and can never stand trial, we have a duty to investigate by the same standards that we would if he was alive. In an investigation, there is no room for speculation. Every piece of information we uncovered and received was analyzed, fact-checked and corroborated in order to assess the weight, validity and value of the information. Our investigative inquiries, actions and standards also centred on gathering evidence to determine what role any individual may have played in terms of having knowledge of the gunman's plan or having assisted him in any way. In light of the evidence gathered during the course of the investigation, today we have charged three people in relation to providing the gunman with ammunition.*
>
> *Throughout the investigation, we have been mindful that when we release information publicly, it causes distress for families and others closely*

associated with those who lost their lives or were injured. Through the assigned RCMP Family Liaison Officers, families have been notified of these charges. The gunman's relationships with others was very much a part of this investigation and, as with every piece of information, were analyzed as we pieced together the gunman's actions, motives and the potential for others' involvement. As a police agency we cannot, however, dismiss evidence from the investigation that others contributed to the incidents by providing the gunman with the ammunition he used on April 18 and 19.

It always bothered me that the statement they made about the newly bought bullets were the ones that were actually used. Gabriel had an ammunition bin full of bullets already, and his guns were always loaded. That said, I have absolutely no doubt that with or without the last purchased bullets, the fate of all would have remained the same.

The following offences: between the 17th day of March and 18th day of April 2020, unlawfully, transferred ammunition, specifically, .223 caliber Remington cartridges and .40 caliber Smith and Wesson cartridges, contrary to Section 101 of the Criminal Code.

They laid charges against me, my brother, and my brother-in-law.

"Based on the investigation to date in which those charged co-operated, these individuals had no prior knowledge of the gunman's actions on April 18 and 19," said Supt. Campbell in the statement. "In addition, investigators have determined the ammunition was purchased and trafficked in Nova Scotia."

Our family had fully co-operated with the RCMP since April 19, eight months ago, when they interviewed every member about their relationship with Gabriel and quizzed us on how he got the guns and ammunition. Because we shared everything without hesitation including our phones, dates, times, the charges felt personal and malicious. I'm not even sure who knew he didn't have a firearms licence or understood what that truly meant. Regardless, we had unwittingly implicated ourselves. None of us helped Gabriel get his guns or knew anything about what he may have been planning or why that fateful April 2020.

Call me naïve, but I honestly didn't know the laws around guns and ammunition. I never, ever thought my family would face a criminal record for doing me a favour. My brother and brother-in-law were both lawful hunters. While ignorance is no excuse, the decision to actually charge us given Gabriel's evil history, seemed like a diversion tactic. Our lawyer said it was highly unusual to lay charges, particularly when the family was fully transparent and co-operative during the entirety of the investigation. It confused us even more as the RCMP publicly stated we had no involvement or culpability in Gabriel's criminal actions.

When I had time to think about the nightmare unfolding, I became angry. We now faced charges that carried a penalty of up to five years in jail. I felt as though they needed someone to blame for the massacre. The families, the public, and the media demanded a public inquiry into the RCMP's handling of events that day. In the days that followed, some people recognized that the charges were a timely deflection from the storm that had engulfed the RCMP. To me, it was more proof that as an abused woman, I couldn't trust the police to help keep me and my family safe. Over the years, the police did nothing when strangers and friends reported Gabriel's illegal behaviour, including possession of illegal firearms and domestic abuse. That would all come out during the public inquiry, but for now, our family remained the only living culprits.

S/Sgt. Vardy interviewed Sean Cologne, Gabriel's closest friend for the past two decades. Sean had given him a handgun as a gift for the work Gabriel had done around his Maine home, but the RCMP did not build a case against him, as he was out of their jurisdiction. Agents with the U.S. Bureau of Alcohol, Tobacco, and Firearms and Explosives spoke to him as well, but he was never charged.

Within weeks, the RCMP's actions had polarized people even more and seemed to fuel the families' anger that no one was being held accountable. The families' lawyer, Robert Pineo, told the CBC media they were "relieved" charges were laid against us. "They've felt throughout that this was a major piece of the puzzle that was missing. Through circumstantial evidence and some information from the community, [they] have felt there was some involvement beyond the killer himself," said Pineo. "So this information has helped put their minds at ease, to a point."

The charges galvanized a belief that I had some responsibility in what Gabriel had done. I was publicly crucified. Much later, RCMP officers would acknowledge they expected backlash against me. "In terms of domestic violence victims, victim-blaming, I thought that would be a significant issue that would need to be addressed," RCMP Chief Superintendent Darren Campbell would later testify at a public inquiry.

I will never get over the pain of our good family name being connected so wrongly to *Gabriel's* atrocities. It cost us immeasurably, both emotionally and financially. Feelings of guilt and shame overwhelmed me as the year ended. The support I'd received from Constable Wayne (Skipper) Bent as a victim of a crime stopped, as well as any help from the Red Cross. It hurts to be publicly vilified for something I didn't do. Up until now, I had focused on my health and well-being. But now I felt hopeless as a possible trial loomed. Were it not for the safe shelter of my sister's home, I would have been destitute.

Not since my childhood had I felt so alone. It was one thing for Gabriel's actions to impact me, but the burden of my choices hurting my family left me feeling responsible and devastated. To this day, our relationship has been affected by the criminal charges. That singular decision set in motion a tailspin and eventual crippling of my emotional and mental health. Though I survived years of abuse by my spouse, my innocence would forever be questioned by those desperate for insight into the truth that died with the only person who knew it.

My sister Janice and my niece, Stephanie, watched Facebook blow up along with the media headlines. The threats toward me escalated after the charges, enough that they were worried about my safety.

You didn't have to look far to find posts about me: "Any decent human being would have tried to stop Wortman, not 'hide in the woods' for eight hours." "She's as guilty as he was," wrote another.

The "witchification" of me had already begun.

18

Legal Peril

This part of my life remains the most complicated. I cannot express where I would be were it not for my family, and in particular my sister Maureen, who became my most trusted advocate. My mental health was so fragile that I was incapable of managing my own needs to survive the aftermath. Both she and Janice handled everything. Janice immediately took leave from her banking career to support my well-being and her own. Maureen went on medical leave from her provincial government position, retiring a year later. Along with caring for me, my legal needs became Maureen's full-time job.

As challenging as my life had become following the mass shooting, I had zero ability to navigate the legal system that bound my entire family after the charges were laid. To say it was formidable is beyond understatement. Maureen became my interpreter-of-sorts when meeting with so many lawyers. I was so overwhelmed and suffering from severe PTSD. She did her best to help me understand, but would often have to repeat herself or remind me days later as my brain could not process or retain much.

MAUREEN:

I HAD NO idea how daunting it would be as a layperson, learning about federal and provincial law in real time as my sister's future hung in the balance. I can't describe the pressure of that onerous responsibility. Though I had administrative experience in my career, this education would be the most consequential of my life.

From the outset, we had to hire a criminal lawyer. The depravity of Gabriel's shooting spree was unprecedented in Canada and Lisa, as his common-law spouse, was the closest person to him. Regardless of her innocence, she needed legal protection. This would be my first exposure to a justice system that I once held in the highest esteem.

Immediately following Gabriel's rampage, a trusted friend recommended James Lockyer. As the lawsuits mounted, it became clear that it was a smart move. I expected to have to leave an awkward message, but Mr. Lockyer personally answered with a disarming English accent. He took control immediately. Though he gently summarized his concerns to Lisa over the phone, he also conveyed a fierce protection of her rights. We knew then, he was the one. I saw a relief in Lisa's body when she hung up. His command of the criminal legal system and experience were undeniable. For the first time, she felt protected.

The public's judgment started when we hired a Toronto lawyer. To some people in our seaside province, it was a sign of guilt. Who calls in the bigwigs from Toronto if they have nothing to hide? Just one of the many judgments that aired on local talk shows.

The fact that Lockyer practised in Toronto proved beneficial, as having someone at arm's length further protected Lisa's privacy. Local media were relentless in covering the details of the soon-to-be international story. To Lisa and the families at the centre of this devastating event, it was not just a sensational story; this was our lives tossed into chaos.

Lisa was the sole beneficiary of Gabriel's estate, as he stipulated in his will. My partner and I witnessed him sign it on March 29, 2011. I was unfamiliar with probate law, so Lisa also had to hire a civil lawyer to advise on the next steps. We chose Peter Rumscheidt of Weldon McInnis in Dartmouth. Peter explained that given the extraordinary circumstances, Lisa would need to relinquish her role as executor in order to place a claim against the estate (valued at $2.1 million by the public trustee).

Robert Pineo, the lawyer for the victims' families, laid claim to the estate for damages and destruction of property. Though we were unable to communicate directly, both parties' lawyers exchanged communication about the claims. Since Lisa was with Gabriel for almost twenty years and contributed to assets, they agreed to bring all the claims together before a judge. This would simplify the process and allow all claimants a portion of the estate.

Rumscheidt applied for what was called an "unjust enrichment" claim on Lisa's behalf. This recognized that Lisa should not be negatively impacted by Gabriel's actions. Because of his excessively controlling nature, the denture business and everything else they acquired and matured while together were registered in Gabriel's name alone. Lisa's contributions to their business and lifestyle were significant, and had she not laid claim, she would stand to lose all assets.

The second of Lisa's claims was for assault, battery, false imprisonment, and intentional infliction of mental suffering related to the violence of that night. Lisa had almost died at his hands, and the assault left her with permanent injuries, most significantly, severe PTSD.

As the lawsuits made their way through the courts, we were reminded by James Lockyer not to speak with anyone; unfortunately, this included the family members of those murdered. Our human compulsion to reach out and comfort one another in our time of need became collateral damage; lines had been drawn. Consumed by the magnitude of what was happening, we focused on Lisa.

Within weeks of being charged, the families added Lisa, our brother, and brother-in-law to a class action suit they had begun. The court documents filed with the Supreme Court of Canada alleged that Lisa and two family members "knew about and facilitated Wortman's preparations," despite the fact the RCMP had stated their investigation concluded that none of us had any knowledge of what Gabriel was going to do with the ammunition. They made headlines for weeks just before Christmas. The charges, above everything else Lisa had endured, tested her will to live: she became suicidal. We had to intervene. The doctor increased her medication, and Janice and I kept vigil. We had never seen her so depressed. There were podcasts sharing conspiracy theories, which became the twisted truth for many people. Lisa felt awful for the families who just wanted answers.

* * *

Before 2020 ended, Lisa now needed to defend herself against this dubious charge. Compounded lawyer fees burdened Lisa's only form of income since the massacre. Her line of credit debt grew, and her legal troubles didn't end there.

Were it not for Jessica Zita, James Lockyer's associate, who took over the day-to-day of her case, I honestly believe we would have lost Lisa. Though an incredible criminal lawyer, it was Jessica's humanity that revived Lisa. Jessica's authentic compassion and empathy comforted Lisa. The evidentiary facts and understanding of the justice system gave us renewed hope that we were struggling to find during that torturous time. While the legal process played out, Lisa had to hire another lawyer to challenge the civil suit she now faced. With no money or income, Lisa relied on her line of credit to provide legal retainers.

Lisa's mental health was already deteriorating and the financial hardship she faced without a job and no income to pay for her defence left her feeling destitute. Since she had lost most of her clothing and other valuables in the fire, she was, in every way, literally starting over.

We anticipated the Red Cross's Stronger Together Fund that raised $6.2 million for those affected by the mass casualty would include helping Lisa with her ongoing treatment and future livelihood needs. The Red Cross initially offered to help pay for Lisa's immediate medical and daily care needs, but as soon as Lisa faced charges, all Red Cross communication and support stopped. As single mothers, Janice and I offered all we could, but beyond essentials, we could not help Lisa financially. We could all share my home, so we were still much better off than most.

On Lisa's behalf, Janice and I applied for and received a modest spousal death benefit, and a year later, she was granted long-term disability support. This obviously could not cover her current legal debt, but did offer relief for daily needs. Throughout this entire ordeal we often talked of the most disenfranchised who face similar circumstances of intimate partner violence: "Can you imagine going through this if you were totally on your own?" At least we had each other and the loving support of so many friends and family.

Even strangers offered to create a GoFundMe for Lisa. As appreciative as she was, Lisa just didn't feel right about it when so many families lost loved ones, and she still had hers. Gabriel's estate would be stalled, as the class action was backed up in the court queue. The bureaucracy of all the legal cases was unbearable as weeks and months passed into year after year. Lisa's legal fees now exceeded $75,000, and she hadn't been to trial yet.

Part of the legal proceedings included interviews with Lisa, to inform a forensic assessment of her mental state. Dr. Peter Jaffe, a world-renowned expert on domestic violence and coercive control, was hired. He criticized the criminal charges laid by an organization sworn to protect when describing the tenets of coercive control in his assessment on January 10, 2022:

> *Ms. Banfield saw firsthand the power that Mr. Wortman had and the failure of anyone to hold him accountable . . . Mr. Wortman's uncle witnessed a serious assault and did nothing. Neighbours who called the RCMP out of concern for her left the jurisdiction because of concern over their own safety. When Mr. Wortman said he was going to go shoot his parents, there was reportedly minimal police follow-up or search for weapons. When there were reports that Mr. Wortman wanted to kill a police officer, there was no reported action taken. When Mr. Wortman assaulted his father while on holidays, there was no action taken. To Ms. Banfield, Mr. Wortman appeared above the law and could easily manipulate the authorities and the system . . . As with many victims of domestic violence, she had no place to turn to as the years went by without an external intervention.*
>
> *In my opinion, from Ms. Banfield's perspective, she had no choice than to pick up the ammunition for Mr. Wortman because of the power and control he had over her. She was especially compliant at this time. COVID-19 had increased her isolation and made him more desperate and paranoid. She lived in fear of him, and in her mind, compliance was her only choice. She was not capable of independent thought. He often told her not to think and just do what he wanted. She was complying with a man who hoarded and collected everything from police cars, motorcycles, firearms, and ammunition. She did not foresee danger to others by helping him obtain more ammunition. She never realized the depth of violence he was capable of.*[13]

19

Validation at a Cost: Facing a Public Inquiry

JULY 15, 2022

THE MASS CASUALTY Commission team led by lawyers Gillian Hnatiw and Emily Hill with the lead investigator, Elizabeth Montgomery, had previously interviewed me for fourteen hours during five lengthy interviews in previous weeks. I felt comfortable with them. Though they were bound by strict mandates, they were kind and respectful to me and my family throughout those sessions, which often caused me to break down and reignited the night terrors of that tragic anniversary weekend.

I awoke with anxiety. Scared but determined, I felt I needed to speak publicly after years of being advised to remain silent because of pending lawsuits. Curious Nova Scotians, the media, angry families of the twenty-two victims—all had waited more than two years to hear what happened that first night. I hadn't been able to talk to anyone publicly, especially the media. I had no experience with public speaking, nor did I want to, but the families deserved to have their questions answered. I understood that. What Gabriel did was evil, and part of me empathized with how they needed to blame someone. He was Canada's worst mass shooter and I was his common-law spouse. Yet

I also wanted to face the detractors and doubters who had spun my harrowing escape into a wild conspiracy theory that I somehow knew what Gabriel had planned or, worse, participated in it. The time to set the record straight had come.

The public inquiry hearings for the Mass Casualty Commission took place at a Marriott Hotel on the Halifax waterfront. That morning hundreds of people and the national media showed up to listen to my every word. The support I felt from the commission staff gave me strength. They had offered for me to do a video appearance because of the trauma I still suffered. I declined because I felt the need to be face-to-face with all those directly impacted.

My only request was that my sisters be allowed to sit by my side and that Gillian be the only one to ask me questions. I had a sense of safety with her. Though I didn't have any problems answering any questions from the families' lawyers, this wasn't a court situation, and I didn't want to feel attacked, given this was the first time I would be speaking in public. The commission denied direct cross-examination and reiterated that any lawyer could ask questions on behalf of their clients via Gillian.

In advance of my testimony, some people were angry and wanted answers the RCMP hadn't provided. The commission was so concerned for my safety that they provided security for me and my sisters. That summer morning, a black SUV showed up at our door. I am from Beaver Bank, Nova Scotia: I had a designated security detail. I felt like I was in a movie. It was surreal.

The driver's earpiece freaked me out a bit. As we approached the hotel, he spoke through his device and, like clockwork, staff moved pylons as our car pulled into a side alley.

Maureen, Janice, and I entered, holding onto each other. They escorted us through the back door of the hotel then crammed into the loading dock elevator. Security guided us through the kitchen toward another elevator. As the two security men in dark suits directed orders through their earpieces, I was a ball of nerves. My body shook and I clenched my jaw to stop my teeth from chattering as we rode upstairs to a private room to wait to testify. When the knock came, indicating it was my turn, we huddled together and prayed. My sisters told me they loved me and that we would get through this together. Prayers have always helped me find the strength to stay focused. I quickly grabbed some Kleenex before being led to the event space filled with vetted spectators, media, families of those murdered, and their respective lawyers.

Before I was ushered onto the stage, people lined up to walk through metal detectors. A police dog sniffed bags. It really hit me. My life was now a public spectacle: Our photos from over the years and intimate details of my life were now part of a public inquiry and internet infamy. The commission released so much about my life with Gabriel and his violence toward me, I felt exposed and vulnerable. The large screen posted images for everyone to see. Though I felt completely out of body, I tried to stay emotionally grounded and focused on Gillian.

As we walked onto the stage and took our seats at a small table with a microphone, I briefly looked at the hundreds of people in the grand ballroom of the hotel. Some of them were clearly angry, standing up with their arms folded over their chests in disdain. Their visible hostility unnerved me, but I also knew they were in pain and I wanted to help. I hoped I could answer their questions.

Then I spotted Denise, my bestie since childhood, and other close friends and family members sitting in the front row of the stage. I gulped down the fear and swallowed hard. There were other supporters in the room. "Women's outreach groups were there," Denise later recalled. "We're so proud of you!" shouted women with placards that read, "We're here for you."

I learned that one organization, Adsum for Women and Children, had posted a statement supporting me as well: "Lisa Banfield is not responsible for the violent actions of the perpetrator committed in April 2020. Lisa is a survivor of decades of abuse and carries no blame."

"It was so tough for me to see her and her sisters up there," said Denise. "This thing has been so surreal. To be up there in front of the world, she was so brave, she was shaking but she held her own. Thank God."

The public session began at 9:30 a.m. The names of the people whose lives were taken and also those harmed by Gabriel were posted on the screen as the proceedings got underway. The Mass Casualty Commission was overseen by Michael MacDonald (a retired chief justice of Nova Scotia), Leanne Fitch (a retired New Brunswick police officer), and Commissioner Kim Stanton (a Toronto lawyer with experience in intimate partner violence). Gillian Hnatiw would be asking the questions. She began the session by saying, "In the spring of 2020, the images were not selected or retained by the RCMP and they only made their way to the commission as part of the materials provided by Ms. Banfield. All of these materials are now in the public record and they form an important part of the commission's investigation to date."

My sisters sat on either side of me at the conference table. As big as that moment was, I felt small. I focused on Gillian. She opened by summarizing previous witnesses who testified about the connections between mass shootings and gender-based violence in the context of rural communities in Atlantic Canada. Brenda Forbes—my former neighbour from Portapique, who I hadn't talked to since she left Nova Scotia years ago—had also testified about Gabriel's violent behaviour. I couldn't bear to watch the earlier hearings, so my sisters had filled me in on what people said about me and Gabriel. It was hard to absorb, especially the long-term affairs he had that I didn't know about. For the first time, I heard of his deplorable actions: how he intimidated and threatened marginalized women in exchange for sexual favours and traded denture services for "other services." Once confronted with the truth, I could no longer deny Gabriel's depravity. I began to mentally separate from him.

"All this information helps us to focus on possible pathways for prevention, intervention and lessons to be learned as we work to make recommendations to help make our communities safer in the future," Gillian said, setting the context for those who hadn't paid attention until that day.

As part of the trauma-informed process, I would not be directly cross-examined by any lawyers other than the commission team, a controversial policy that upset the victims' families.

I took the Bible and swore to tell the truth, which I did. She asked about my family, my first date with Gabriel, and then got me to describe our cottage at 200 Portapique Beach Road and our nearby warehouse on 136 Orchard Beach Drive. The photos I had provided to the police and commission flashed up on the screen. By mid-morning, Gillian zeroed in on Gabriel's obsession with buying four decommissioned police cars during 2019. I described the white Ford Taurus vehicles in detail and testified that he got them from Nova Scotia Crown Assets. We drove two of them, one with stripes and one without. Gabriel liked driving them because it made him feel powerful.

A third, undriveable one, was used for parts, and the fourth, now-infamous replica, he stored in our warehouse. Gillian wanted to know where Gabriel got the materials and decals to make the police car look like a replica RCMP vehicle; he told me he got them from the internet and a guy from Crown Assets. She asked me why he built it. I told her he wanted the replica for parties, for show. It was not a registered vehicle, so it could not be driven. At one point Gabriel told me he wanted to have the names of fallen RCMP officers on the hood and perhaps be featured in parades. Pictures I had provided appeared on the screen that showed the inside of the car he had locked me in on April 18 and the Plexiglas that slid open, which I had crawled through. For some reason, the police never released these to the commission as evidence of my story, but the commission entered them as exhibits.

"Did you have any concerns about the fact that he seemed to have a fully marked RCMP vehicle at his disposal?" Gillian asked.

"Yes," I said. I had concerns and raised them with Gabriel. "'You need to find out if you're even allowed to have this,' I said, and he's like, 'Oh, yeah, I'll—.' And I said, 'If you don't, I'll call and ask them so you don't have to worry about it.' And he's like, 'No, Lisa, don't. I will look after it.' So then I would ask him again, 'Did you find out if you can?' And he said he went to a Crown prosecutor, and they said, 'As long as you don't drive it.'" It was the same response he gave to others as well.

I never saw Gabriel drive the replica RCMP car. When Gillian asked if I thought he would drive it, I told her no.

The next question left the room gasping at my response.

"Do you know who Bruce Gilmour is?"

"Yes."

"OK, who is he?"

"From Mercedes. I think he's the manager from Mercedes."

Gillian continued, "In a statement to the commission, Mr. Gilmour said that sometime in the winter of 2020, we think January, he suggests, January 30, 2020, that he saw the perpetrator drop you off at the Mercedes dealership in the fully decked-out RCMP car."

"Never happened; it would have been the one with the stripes."

Gillian paused. "And so, Mr. Gilmour was quite firm in his recollection that he provided to the commission."

Without hesitation, I answered, "I'm firm in mine." I knew the truth. I had never been in the replica RCMP car.

For the next twelve seconds, the room collectively hushed. I felt the audience hadn't anticipated my answer to be as sharp as it sounded. Up until then, I felt uneasy, and my voice appeared shaky and quiet. Afterwards, my sisters said, it was the one moment they heard conviction in my voice. They told me how proud they were that I stood up for myself at that moment.

Gabriel owned a fake police badge that prompted many questions, and I explained he did use it to get discounts in Maine: "It looked like a police badge, but it was actually an ambulance badge. He would use it if we went to hotels."

Gabriel collected uniforms, including one of a firefighter and a bus driver. He owned black RCMP pants with the stripes down the leg and a red serge jacket, given to him by his uncle Chris, a retired RCMP officer, which was too small for Gabriel. He also had a corrections officer uniform and set of handcuffs he got from his friend Sean McLeod, one of the victims. He kept them in a nightstand; the same ones he used on me that night.

"He collected things. My whole life with Gabriel, he would collect things: motorbikes, cars, uniforms, toilet paper, bulk stuff and as abnormal as that sounds, it was normal to me because that was my whole life with him, if that makes sense."

Gillian pressed me again by asking if Gabriel would impersonate a police officer with the badge, car, and pieces of a uniform. I didn't ever see him do that. It never crossed my mind that he would do such a thing. I testified about his guns, which I believe he got while in the States with his friend Sean. I never wanted anything to do with guns and insisted he never bring them across the border with me in the vehicle.

"I never reported him. I know it doesn't make sense. He was my partner and I was afraid of him. There were a couple of times during a fight he would put a gun to my head to scare me. He said that he could blow my head off. I said, 'I'm not going to say anything to anyone.'"

Gillan followed up, "So given that you were scared and that he sometimes used those firearms to threaten you, why didn't you think of calling the police and asking them to come get those guns?"

It was a fair question. Why didn't I call the police over the years? I couldn't trust what he would do. Police, neighbours, and even my family couldn't protect me. Whenever I threatened to leave, Gabriel warned me that I would regret it. It felt dangerous not only for me but for those I loved. I believed to my core that I was alone in this; no one but God could keep me safe.

To those who think it's easy to leave, all I can say is you'd have to be in my shoes and under his complete and total control to understand. I wept as Gillian asked me this.

"No," I testified, "I never thought of calling the police. I feared what he would do, and grown men who knew he had guns didn't say anything either. They were scared of him, so what am I going to do?" This response made headlines the next day.

By the afternoon, there were fewer people there, as some of the families of the victims left for the day, frustrated by the process. They wanted the opportunity to ask me questions directly and to cross-examine me. The trauma-informed parameters for all witness testimony were outlined well in advance. Sadly, Pineo and his team of lawyers opted to ask nothing, since they couldn't question me directly or cross-examine me. Instead, they left.

Some questions brought forward through other participants focused on April 18, and what I told investigators happened that fateful night. I testified I did hear gunshots throughout the night, while I crawled through the woods and when I hid inside the tree trunk. I repeated what I'd told the RCMP: the sound of people swearing and then shots followed by silence.

When Gillian asked me if I agreed with Brenda's assessment that I was "the perpetrator's Barbie doll" of whom he had full control,

I agreed—even though I felt humiliated by the description. She also wanted to know if I suspected Gabriel would plan a mass casualty event. "No." That was never a consideration; I had no idea he would do such a thing. To me, he was paranoid during COVID. He talked like a crazy person; I didn't want to hear it. I was horrified by what he had done.

The most emotionally difficult part was the questions about why Gabriel would target certain people that night, or if I knew about any grievances he had with our neighbours in Portapique, including some who I didn't personally know. I wish I could have offered the families something, but I had absolutely no idea about his intentions or his reasons for killing any of them.

"Is it possible that he had gone to their home looking for you?"

"This haunts me, even today, because I feel he was targeting me and my family. If I didn't get out of that car, I think, would any of those people have died? So that's something that haunts me all the time because I feel that he was looking for me in the beginning."

I knew so little about the people Gabriel murdered; I'm sure it was discouraging for their loved ones who hoped I could share more insight into his reasons for killing their family members. I don't know why to this day.

During breaks, the commission team met with the lawyers to elicit any final questions for me. I barely held it together. My voice shook and cracked as I tried to speak free of emotion. Overwhelmed by the day and the scrutiny, my fatigue started showing. Gillian finished by asking if the rumours in the media and online had impacted my mental health.

Here's what I said:

"In so many ways, it has impacted myself and my family because people don't know who we are. And the fact that people would think I would have anything to do with this—like, our family, you know, feels for all those people and we're not angry because if it was my family, I would feel the same way. But it's just angering because *he* did this, and I didn't. And I would never contribute to anything like that. It's scary to think that people are angry and that somebody could come after me or my family if they think that we had anything to do with it."

Her final question was about what would have helped me: "You've described at a number of points in your evidence today and in your interviews with the commission that there were those in the community who observed the assaults, who, as you described, were also afraid of him. If you had more support from the community, do you think that it would have made a difference in your ability to either seek help or leave the relationship?"

I shook my head. "I don't think I would have, just because he threatened my family, so it's one thing that I can hide or get help, but what are they all going to do? I couldn't take the risk, knowing that he could come after any of my family."

I would answer it the same way today. I do wonder if the police had interviewed me during that first assault and held him accountable, whether my life would have taken a different turn? *Looking back now, I wish they had.*

When asked if I needed more support, I looked at my sisters. "If it wasn't for my family, I don't know where I'd be living, what I would be doing. And it's hard for me to say this, because I know I'm here, and my family's here, and there are so many people that aren't here. I don't want to complain about what I don't have."

We ended at 5:03 p.m. with Justice MacDonald turning to face me. He sincerely thanked me for coming and acknowledged my sisters' support: "This has been a very difficult day for many. The pain and hurt here today have been palatable and it emanates everywhere. But it has been an especially difficult day for you, Ms. Banfield. And I wanted to thank you for assisting us, even though it meant you yet again having to relive some more of the horrific ordeals you went through, and we are especially grateful for that. You've shown courage by coming here and again, we are thankful. Maureen and Janice, you are wonderful siblings. Thank you for being there for your sister, which meant your sister was here for us."

We exited the room.

Following my testimony, trauma counsellors from Adsum for Women and Children asked if they could leave their card for support. I was emotionally exhausted but wanted to thank them personally for their support. Security led them to my suite, and we shared a moment that I appreciate and value to this day. My sisters and I collapsed into each other's arms. This chapter was done. I was proud of myself for providing all I could to help and have no regrets in participating in the inquiry's important work.

As the first newscasts ran pictures of me weeping and apologizing, and some family members walking out, would they ever feel peace or comfort? I pray they will. I tried to share what I could about what happened, but of course, they wanted to know why he did this—questions without answers, the whys, none of us will ever know. I doubt if any of us will ever find closure, but I do pray for peace.

As I re-read my testimony five years later, I noticed how often I kept saying, "I'm sorry."

"Sorry" as I tried to explain my thinking during stressful times with Gabriel;

"Sorry" for having to clarify why I lied to the police about having guns in the house;

"Sorry" I stayed;

"Sorry" I didn't report his abuse;

"Sorry" I had no idea what he was planning.

That night, Janice read me a Facebook post she received. I am choosing to share this stranger's words because they still gives me strength, knowing there are women who will understand what I've lived through:

> *God love you girls . . . I am sure you are exhausted from the stressful day. Lisa did an amazing job, I had tears in my eyes for most of her testimony. Please know that there are many of us who care and are supportive of Lisa and you girls. I will continue to speak out in support of your brave courageous sister. The behaviour of those present was shameful. I don't know what more they all want from your sister, she gave her all today. If you ever need anyone to help with anything, please reach out to me. I am a spousal abuse survivor myself and know how alone one can feel. No one knows until you actually live through it. Hope you can all relax tonight and look after yourselves well. Hugs*

After my testimony, the headlines seemed to soften, but there were still some people who doubted me. Some alternative media outlets still fed conspiracy theories that Gabriel was an undercover cop or that I knew what he was planning and participated in the murders. One specific article signaled a change in the past narrative of condemnation. It totally shifted the public's perception. The reporter dared to ask: Why was I being "witchified"?

From "The Witchification of Lisa Banfield" by Tim Bousquet in the *Halifax Examiner*, July 17, 2022:

> *There is a campaign of lies, innuendo, misogyny, and hatred directed against Lisa Banfield. The goal, apparently, is to destroy her. After the murders, Banfield completely co-operated with investigators . . . sat down for five multi-hour interviews with Mass Casualty Commission investigators . . . All of the above—transcripts of each of the interviews, email and phone records, etc.—is available publicly; anyone can read them. As painful and embarrassing as that would be for anyone, Lisa Banfield's*

> *life is an open book . . . Even as the murders were occurring, it was Banfield who alerted the RCMP to the reality of the fake police car (before that, police seemed incapable of understanding what other witnesses were plainly telling them) . . . (It's surely not Banfield's fault that police then failed to alert the public about the car.) . . . [She is] a modern-day witch, and they are on a witch hunt . . . and ultimately unknowable reasons for the murders of April 2020 are assigned to a woman, who is to take responsibility for the sins of a man.*[14]

* * *

On March 30, 2023—almost three years after Gabriel's rampage—we got a phone call from my lawyers. The commission was about to release their final report, titled *Turning the Tide Together.* My lawyers, James Lockyer and Jessica Zita, pored over the 130 recommendations contained in the report, many related to intimate-partner violence.

I appreciated all the thought that went into the report and the efforts to change the justice system. But on that day, I felt relief when Chief Justice MacDonald said he'd heard and believed me. After testimony from sixty-one witnesses and interviews with over two hundred and thirty people, he concluded, "It is clear for nineteen years Lisa Banfield was abused by her spouse, and it culminated on April 18. We highlight that she was clearly the first victim, and our view, as stated in the report, is that she ought to have been immediately recognized as such."

The commission found critical gaps in the RCMP response and public communications to warn people Gabriel was still on the loose after lighting fires and killing people. Whether they could have prevented even some of the murders is an issue that still reverberates today. Commissioner Kim Stanton called out the RCMP for its decision to interview me right after I emerged from the woods, and pointed out that even in those first hours I wasn't believed or taken seriously when I warned police about the "exact" replica RCMP car. The fact that I was criminally charged by the RCMP following interviews, without my lawyer present and while also heavily medicated, was dubious and touched off a wave of "revictimization."

> *As Ms. Banfield's testimony reveals, the consequences of being criminally charged proved dire for her. She became the target of, and defendant to, the families' class action lawsuit, which alleged that she was responsible for the unimaginable suffering caused by the perpetrator. Perhaps most devastating, she became publicly vilified with the narrative that she was somehow responsible for the mass casualty (despite the same RCMP confirming that their investigation revealed no such responsibility). In the end, Ms. Banfield found herself reviled and destitute.*

The commissioners concluded that I never saw myself as the same level of victim as the families of the twenty-two dead people, including widower Nick Beaton, who also lost his unborn child.

"Not victim enough" rang so true. I believed God spared me. I'm a survivor who found my voice to speak the truth of my life with Gabriel. I still had to find my inner resilience to face the legal challenges and blame that hung over me.

POST INQUIRY – WHAT HAPPENED

Of the commission's one hundred and thirty recommendations, more than half focused on the RCMP and the decisions they made during the thirteen hours Gabriel Wortman was on the loose. The RCMP critical-incident response was hindered by system-wide poor communication and failures of coordination. The RCMP's failure to publicly share accurate and timely information, including information about the perpetrator's replica RCMP cruiser and disguise, deprived community members of the opportunity to evaluate risks to their safety and to take measures to better protect themselves.

The deadliest mass shooter in Canada appeared to have no plan or list during April 18 and 19. "He had made preparations, but we cannot conclude he made a plan," they wrote. Some victims were unknown to him. "Some of the perpetrator's actions—in particular, the motivation for his violent rampage—are unknown at this time and likely will remain so forever."

KEY FINDINGS RELATED TO LISA BANFIELD AND GABRIEL WORTMAN:[15]

- Over many years, the perpetrator's pattern of violent and intimidating behaviours and illegal acquisition of firearms gave rise to numerous red flags and missed opportunities for prevention and intervention.
- There was intergenerational violence in the perpetrator's family. The perpetrator was physically and emotionally abused as a child and, as an adult, he was violent toward his father.
- The perpetrator's pattern of violent and intimidating behaviour was facilitated by the power and privilege he experienced as a white man with professional status and substantial means.
- The perpetrator's illegal acquisition of firearms provided him with the means to carry out the mass casualty. Despite many red flags, existing enforcement practices were ineffective in preventing the perpetrator from illegally acquiring and possessing these firearms and from smuggling them across the land border between the United States and Canada.
- He had shown some of these firearms to several individuals, including his family, his neighbours, and members of Ms. Banfield's

family. On three occasions, someone reported his possession of firearms to the police.

- Many community residents knew about the perpetrator's replica RCMP cruiser, but no one reported its existence to authorities.
- Despite widespread community knowledge of the perpetrator's violent and otherwise illegal, intimidating, and predatory behaviour over a number of years, there were impediments to safely reporting concerns, including a fear of retaliation, ineffective access points, and a lack of faith in an adequate police response.
- The Commission cannot conclude on the available evidence that the perpetrator was a paid police informant. The Commission cannot conclude on the available evidence that the perpetrator was involved in the purchase or sale of drugs, in money laundering, or in organized crime.
- In the six weeks before the mass casualty, the perpetrator further isolated his common law spouse from her family as his behaviour became erratic and increasingly concerning to her.
- The mass casualty began before 10:00 p.m. on April 18, 2020, with the perpetrator's violent assault of Lisa Banfield in the Portapique cottage. Physical evidence found by RCMP investigators corroborates her account.
- The perpetrator inflicted serious injuries on Ms. Banfield, including fractures to her ribs and lumbar spine, before setting the cottage on fire and forcing her to accompany him to his nearby warehouse.
- The RCMP did not treat Lisa Banfield as a surviving victim of the mass casualty; that is, as an important witness who required careful debriefing and who would need support services.

The RCMP's treatment of Lisa Banfield during the RCMP's H-Strong investigation is an example of the kind of revictimization that makes it less likely that women survivors of gender-based violence will seek help from police. The victim blaming and hyper-responsibilization (holding of an individual to higher standards than what would typically be expected of the average person) to which Ms. Banfield was subjected by community members reflect myths about "triggers" in a mass casualty and that a woman is responsible for her partner's actions. This reaction also has a chilling effect on other survivors of gender-based violence.

20

Time to Heal

FIVE YEARS LATER

SOME NIGHTS, I STILL dream of Gabriel chasing me, vowing to kill me. I can't get away from him. I wake with my heart pounding, disoriented, and in a lather of sweat. Fear forces me to check the doors to make sure they're locked, even though I know Gabriel is dead. I am still haunted by the "what-ifs." If I had stayed with him that night would anyone have died? Was he going door-to-door hunting for me? During those first few years, I *survived* in a fight or flight state; I felt afraid to go outside because people stared at me.

Although no one has ever confronted me, I find myself vigilantly looking over my shoulder with dread. Facing the public inquiry only intensified my awareness that some people will always view me as a villain. That still hurts, and the ongoing lawsuits erode my sleep reserves. For the past five years I've lived in a crucible: a psychological prison, impenetrable and isolating.

After the Mass Casualty Commission filed its findings, the lawyers representing me and the families worked to negotiate a settlement of Gabriel's $2.1-million estate. A trial scheduled to be held in December 2024 loomed over everything I did. The families' lawyers had added my family as defendants to the class-action lawsuit seeking damages for deaths, property destruction, and injuries back in 2021 when the criminal charges against my family were laid. No one, least of all me, wanted a public trial, but I believed I had a right to some of the estate I helped build. This wasn't about taking money away from the deserving families who had lost so much; it was about fair and equitable division based on these unthinkable circumstances. None of us would ever be compensated for what happened to us, but maybe we could all move past this infamous connection to a man who caused so much pain.

Facing a stalemate, we agreed to meet to try to mediate a settlement. This would be the final opportunity for resolution before going to court. On July 4, 2024, Janice and Maureen joined me for the judicial settlement conference at the Supreme Court of Nova Scotia on the Halifax waterfront.

We sat in awkward silence in the common space outside the court offices while our lawyers exchanged pleasantries awaiting the judge's arrival. The judge overseeing the mediation wanted the parties to find common ground, so he addressed us all to explain the process. "No one will leave here today happy. But if we are open to the process, we could at least agree on a settlement that you could live with and move on with your lives," he said.

After separating us into two rooms, the negotiations began. By the end of that day, we had agreed to a pending settlement. Because of the non-disclosure agreement, I am unable to share details beyond its resolution. The most important thing to me was that my family didn't have to endure a trial. The family representatives agreed to drop the civil suit against me and my family members; otherwise, I would not have accepted their offer; it was worth not having my family endure further public scrutiny. Although the mediation left me dissatisfied, it ended an exhausting and costly process. When the lawyers finalized the paperwork that fall, I no longer had to live on my line of credit. With four years of legal fees debt paid, I could finally breathe.

Expressing my personal sympathy to the families also mattered, regardless of how much they seemed to loathe me. I grieved for them. For years I had been told by my therapist and restorative team not to say the words, "I'm sorry," because I didn't cause this. But as a compassionate person, it never felt right not to acknowledge their pain in the aftermath and offer my sympathy to them.

During the pre-trial deposition with the families' lawyers, Nick Beaton served as the families' representative for the estate trial. For several sessions, I looked at him across the conference table. I couldn't imagine his inconsolable pain of losing his beloved wife to murder while expecting their second child. Kristen Beaton was a continuing care assistant for the Victorian Order of Nurses.

On the last day of my deposition, I decided, *I'm doing it, I'm going to say something*. Though the setting wasn't the place to share my sentiments, I knew there wouldn't be another opportunity to express my personal condolences.

An ordinary, unpretentious man whose life was upended in the most cruel and instantaneous way sat before me in an oversized hoodie and ball cap. His facial hair helped to hide his disdain for me. Nonetheless, I looked him in the eyes. Mr. Beaton was talking to someone else when I walked over and gently put my hand on his shoulder. He turned slightly toward me, "I'm sorry for your loss and for the loss of the other families," I said. He just looked at me and put his head down. I turned and walked away.

Because of mounting pressure to have me participate in the public inquiry, prosecutors had offered me, my brother and my brother-in-law the restorative justice option in exchange for dropping the charges. We accepted the arrangement, clearing the path for me to testify. The process is aimed at understanding and addressing the harms and needs of those affected by crime, and is educational as well as preventative. Because none of us were charged or culpable in the murders, nor could it be proven that the bullets Gabriel used were the ones we purchased, the restorative parameters did not include the harm to the families for their loved ones' murders.

Unfortunately, some families believed they would be involved and be able to address me and my family about the impact of their grief and loss. "I want to meet with them anyway so they can ask any question of me," I offered the facilitator.

"It wouldn't be safe," he told me.

Safe? The word reinforced to me that I would never find peace with some of the victims' family members who continue to question if I knew more than I had told the police. "Some family members are not in a place to be a part of a healing circle at this time," the facilitator continued. "Perhaps in the future, you can offer a healing circle for those wanting closure."

It was as if the system pitted us against each other, an us-versus-them scenario. The week after I appeared at the commission, I returned to provincial court accompanied by my sisters to hear a judge formally dismiss the criminal charges against me.

Our family, like the other twenty-two families, was forever changed by the horror of the massacre. None of us will ever be the same. I still carry so much guilt that my older brother and brother-in-law were caught up in Gabriel's unforgivable rampage. They also had to hire lawyers; the financial and traumatic toll forever changed our family dynamic. There are some relatives who never want to discuss it, or share their experiences, in this book. I understand and respect their wishes and privacy.

I survive not by denying what Gabriel did, but by refusing to wallow in anger and sadness every day. I can't focus on him killing people or the magnitude of his actions. I know I can't change anything that he did, and I am consumed by grief revisiting all of it. It sends me backwards, not forward. How is that helping me? It's not, it keeps me stuck and I don't want to be stuck anymore.

Part of my healing includes holding the RCMP accountable for its manipulative behaviour as a trusted authority, and its inept understanding and practices with regard to domestic violence and coercive control. I shared everything I could with them during the interviews and yet my co-operation resulted in charges being laid and my reputation destroyed. I am suing them for damages. The RCMP admitted publicly that none of us knew Gabriel was planning to use the bullets to murder people. There is no evidence proving that those bullets were used. I believe the RCMP needed to draw attention away from the errors they committed. The commission found that at least thirty-five people knew of Gabriel's gun collection and three separate reports had been made to the police.

I won't ever recover from the pain that compounded my trauma, derailed my healing, destroyed my reputation, and crushed my family. While there is no monetary compensation great enough to repair that harm, their acknowledgement and accountability will go a long way to provide closure to this part of my life.

* * *

I've spent years in therapy from the time I left the hospital, trying to gain some quality of life. My first therapist, Lisa Richardson from the mental health team in Truro, supported me while I was at my lowest point in my life after the massacre. She helped me to see that Gabriel had manipulated me during our entire relationship. Sitting with her and talking, Lisa made me feel safe and reassured me the abuse wasn't my fault.

Because in my darkest moments, you start to think, maybe it *is* my fault. Gabriel would say, "If you didn't do that, I wouldn't have to hit you, it's your fault." I would think, *maybe he was right; maybe if I didn't do that, he wouldn't have hit me.* My brain was spinning. His voice and words constantly churned in my thoughts. I was so confused, wrapped up in whatever he would say. I lost my voice.

One winter day in 2022, I sat in front of a screen on a Zoom call staring at a man who would help change my life. Dr. Jaffe, the psychologist based in Toronto, had worked in his field for forty years with the police and court system. He was different from Lisa, my therapist, as he delved far back into my childhood before discussing my relationship with Gabriel. I spoke freely with him. He had read all the interviews I gave to the RCMP. He recognized my vulnerability when I met Gabriel, a result of growing up with alcoholic parents and experiencing sexual abuse at an early age.

He concluded that I was an easy mark for Gabriel. I lost courage the times I did leave or threatened to leave. Financially, I could try to return to my old job if I left Gabriel, but he would tell me, "You're lucky to have me," putting thoughts in my head that I'm better off to stay with him. The choice to go would impact not just me, but my family, I feared. I would get this visceral pain in my gut. He would drop innuendo whenever I tried, saying, "I know where your family lives . . ." I knew what he could do to me, but what about them?

I told Dr. Jaffe part of me truly believed I could help Gabriel overcome his abusive childhood if I loved him enough to help him heal the broken parts of him. That's when he explained what fawning meant. You think you can love someone in hopes your affection will stop them from abusing you. The next minute, you walk on eggshells trying to read your abuser's moods to avoid retaliation.

Dr. Jaffe understood exactly how I was feeling and helped me make sense of who I had become in order to survive. It's like he'd known me for years. How my whole life had brought me to this point and why I stayed in an abusive relationship for so long.

In his assessment, Dr. Jaffe suggested I was a risk to myself and would need many years of specialized therapy to fully function in society again. It stung to read his report, but he offered me incredible advice and recommended several therapists for the intensive mental health support I required. I called the one in Toronto, but decided in-person would work better. He recommended Shireen Singer, a specialized therapist in Chester, Nova Scotia. When we spoke, it took me just five minutes to know she was my person. I've seen her weekly since then. If it wasn't for her and having a different perspective and outlet to see my broken self, I would be in a hole, perhaps literally.

With her help and my commitment to living past my past, I now accept that I was an abused woman. I never did before. I remember watching *Oprah* and yelling at the television at a woman who wouldn't stand up to her man when he was berating her. "Stand up for yourself," I yelled at her. It's so sad to see women in that situation where they have no hope or faith. How sick is it that I couldn't do what I wanted the woman on TV to do?

During the spring of 2025, I dreaded the fifth anniversary of the massacre. I never watch news stories at this time of year. I am not on social media, so I avoid all public comments about what happened. I relive that fateful day constantly. As April 18 approaches, I withdraw from others, even my sisters. I isolate myself and my thoughts.

My therapist recommended getting away. I tried to plan a trip to physically escape. That didn't work out; I couldn't escape. I couldn't detach from the reality of my life "now" and was exhausted from sinking into the abyss of "then." All the work I'd done with my therapist over the last couple of years prepared me for this long-awaited moment. Letting go was my only way forward.

On April 18, 2025, I awoke, ready to shed any physical connection to Gabriel. It was time to say goodbye. I got my phone and opened the two decades of pictures chronicling my life with him. One by one, I hit *Delete*.

Pictures of our cottage and warehouse. Click. Gone.

Videos of his fiftieth birthday party. Click. Gone.

Messages and emails. Click. Gone.

Every single reminder of our life together. Click. Gone.

And I wasn't done yet.

I took his remaining ashes I'd stored in my bedroom, and with my new-found strength, I released him forever.

My life with Gabriel. Gone.

EPILOGUE

Horizon of Hope

I STARTED OFF as a broken girl. As hard as it is at times, I am doing my best to embrace this transformative journey I am on. The truth is: I am a different person now. I pity *That Girl.* I didn't value or love myself; I didn't matter. Not understanding my worth and not knowing that I am lovable and enough just as I am—that's the power I gave to the man in my life for nineteen years. Sometimes, I'm asked, "What has changed for you?" I have reclaimed my independence, but it's definitely a process. I have worked hard through therapy and will require more to move forward. I've done a lot of reflecting and soul searching about what would make *me* happy. For so long I focused on others' needs and wants, especially the men in my life. It was depleting, and somewhere along the way I lost myself. I was petrified to start over, but living a life of fear with a person who was unstable and abusive is far scarier.

During the RCMP interviews with S/Sgt. Vardy, I was asked how often I was assaulted. I estimated ten times, because I couldn't recall each beating that I erased out of my mind, onto the pages of my journal. For so long I convinced myself that an abused woman got beaten every day. That is why I believed I stayed. I never saw myself as *that* woman. My mistaken belief was that it wouldn't happen again. That he didn't mean to hurt me. If I loved him enough, I could change him. The term "coercive control" has broadened my understanding of abuse to mean "total control over another person." Now, I've come to understand that daily emotional and mental abuse does define my experience. I am a survivor of intimate-partner violence.

Part of my reason for writing this book is to help other women struggling with denial, hoping to change an abuser because you love and want so desperately to help them. My advice to other women is to follow your instincts; your gut doesn't lie. After the first time he hit me, I wish I would have reported him for assault and left for good. I wish I believed my intuition. Instead, I convinced myself: *I can make it work. We can get past this.* I now know, if it happens once, it will happen again and again and again. The truth is, it will never stop without external intervention. If your partner says it's because they were drinking or because you provoked it, or it's your fault, don't believe them. Lean into your gut's truth. You deserve the best of yourself and others.

Unfortunately for me, it took a near-death experience to see all the ways I stayed with someone who hurt me so profoundly. In reading my journals, I prayed to God to show me signs, help me see, and make my path clear. The sad truth is He did. With every record of the humiliation, death-fearing threat, choking, beating, and vile-spewing word, I see now God's message in my own words: "Get Out! Leave! No More! Enough!"—but I did not listen. I would only focus on the good times, the what-ifs, the remember-whens, denying my daily reality. Instead, I prayed, hoped, pretended, ignored, excused, accepted—and, miraculously, thank God, I survived. In the future, the person I'm going to be with will know my story and respect my boundaries. There will never be second chances regarding my worth. I am still working on myself every day. I'm becoming the woman that I am meant to be.

A lot of people ask me, "Are you seeing anyone?" I tell them I need time to focus on myself and to heal. I've always thought that if I were to meet someone else, it would be in God's time. I am blessed because I am alive today and hopeful for a future helping others.

Detailing my journey in this book for others to relate to, and to set the record straight from my perspective, has helped me reflect on the choices I made and will make in the future. I must live with the consequences and use these lessons to strengthen my determination to never devalue my worth as a woman. I am in control of what I want my future to look like. There will always be residual scars but there are many ways to cope and heal. Beyond my family, I discovered unconditional love with my precious little dog, Lilly. We are inseparable. I swear she is human. We calm each other and she has been by my side throughout my healing.

In years to come, when I am strong enough, I hope to share my experience with young women and men. Perhaps save another "Lisa" from losing herself to the needs of others. There are many women's and family shelters that I'd love to support. I feel good helping others; it feeds my soul.

In my low moments, when I falter, I am reminded of the grace I received from Sarah, a stranger from Colchester, Nova Scotia. She wrote me during the darkest time of my life, and I draw inspiration from it often:

To the woman, the whole world can't stop thinking about.

I found myself lost for words while trying to reflect on what the events of this past week has done to our community. To our province. To our nation as a whole. No matter how much I read, or hear about, or how many scenarios I play out in my mind, inevitably my mind always wanders back to you. How amazingly, brave and strong you are. How resourceful and resilient and determined of a woman you are. You escaped and survived a night that, I have no doubt at all, this horrible man intended for you to not make it through.

I cannot begin to imagine what your life must have been like with this man. I'm sure something most people couldn't imagine in their worst nightmares. I cannot begin to imagine the pain, the guilt, the shame, the regret, and the heartache. The excruciating heartache you are dealing with right now. I know it's kept you up at night replaying that night in your mind, every detail.

All of the things YOU did wrong. Or could have done differently. Because that's what abusers train your mind to do. After a while, they don't even have to blame you anymore, you just learned to blame yourself without them saying a word. I know you were conditioned into believing this was love. And that without him, you would be nothing or have nothing. I know this is something that time most likely won't heal but hopefully will make it easier to carry.

I need you to know that you are SO much better than that monster. You're worth SO much more. Even though he told you that you were worthless. That's the only way cowards like him keep amazingly, beautiful, strong, smart and successful women like you around.

Thank you for being so strong, and for helping the police to end this unthinkable rampage. Thank you for fighting to hang on that night. Thank you for inspiring all of us in so many ways about your strength and survival.

This is NOT your fault. Any of it. It never was.

You are a hero.

You are a survivor.

You are free . . .

This is your second chance. And we all stand behind you. When it gets too heavy to carry the burden alone, please reach out and let us take some of the load.

We love you. You are never alone.

Thank you, Sarah. I don't feel alone anymore. My voice is getting stronger too. I am so very blessed and grateful to be alive and free from a life that almost killed me. As a *free* woman, I realize how important it is to be self-sufficient and to know you can be your own rock: strong and solid. I have a deep spiritual belief in God. My devotion to prayer continues to anchor me. Part of my healing will be to reach out and thank all those people who gave me and my family the precious gifts of grace, love, and hope.

To other women wanting to leave abusive relationships, my hope is you love yourself enough to realize *you matter*. I wish we all can experience a moment when we at our core feel heard and seen, even when we are invisible to ourselves. Give yourself grace.

Is there such a thing as healing from a traumatic tragedy? Yes. I hope the love I've received is passed on to those in need. My story isn't over. It feels like I'm creating my own path for the first time in my life. I know I'm going to be OK. I'm learning that until you deal with past trauma, it will follow you into future relationships. The love I seek is already within me.

I know that one day I will be ready to receive healthy love from a true partner. For now, I am finding my voice.

Honouring the Innocent Victims

Tom Bagley: Seventy, father, husband, retired firefighter, leading seaman with the Royal Canadian Navy and the Halifax Stanfield International Airport Fire department

Kristen Beaton: Thirty-three, mother expecting a second child, continuing care assistant with the Victoria Order of Nurses, lived in Onslow Mountain, Colchester County

Greg and Jamie Blair: Greg, Forty-five, Jamie, Forty, a married couple, were devoted hockey parents and grandparents, ran a family business, GB Gas and Energy

Peter and Joy Bond: Peter, Seventy-four, retired truck driver, and Joy, Seventy, a married couple, were parents, grandparents, and great-grandparents

Lillian Campbell: Sixty-five, mother, retired nurse

Corrie Ellison: Forty-two, Truro resident

Gina Goulet: Fifty-four, mother, denturist for twenty-seven years

Frank and Dawn Gulenchyn: a retired married couple from Ontario, were parents and grandparents, living in Portapique

Alanna Jenkins: Thirty-six, Corrections Canada manager, stepmother and nana, from Wentworth

Sean McLeod: Forty-four, Corrections Canada officer, father, grandfather, partner of Alanna Jenkins

Lisa McCully: Forty-nine, elementary school teacher, mother of two, from Portapique

Heather O'Brien: Fifty-five, nurse with the Victorian Order of Nurses, mother and grandmother, from Masstown

The Tuck Family: Jolene Oliver, Thirty-nine, waitress, and **Aaron Tuck**, Forty-five, mechanic from Portapique, parents of **Emily Tuck**, seventeen, a student and fiddler

Constable Heidi Stevenson: Forty-eight, Royal Canadian Mounted Police officer for twenty-three years, wife and mother of two children

Joanne Thomas and John Zahl: John, Seventy, and Joanne, Fifty-nine, a married couple, were parents and grandparents, who retired in Portapique

Joey Webber: Thirty-six, father who lived in Wyses Corner near Shubenacadie

SURVIVORS

Lisa Banfield: Hospitalized with broken ribs and lumbar spine

Constable Chad Morrison: Hospitalized after being shot and wounded by the perpetrator

Andrew MacDonald: He called 911 to report the perpetrator's warehouse on fire and then the Gulenchyn house on fire. Within minutes, the perpetrator pulled up alongside him in the replica RCMP car and shot through the window, hitting Andrew's shoulder and grazing his head.

If You Need Help:

CALL 911

National services and resources

SHELTERS

Sheltersafe.ca:

Provides information and a clickable map to help connect women and their children across Canada with the nearest shelter for safety and support.

Sheltersafe, "If You're A Woman Experiencing Abuse, There is Someone You Can Reach Out to Any Time, Day or Night," *Women's Shelters Canada*, https://sheltersafe.ca/get-help/

FOR WOMEN

iHEAL app:

A free, private, and secure app to help Canadian women who have experienced abuse from a current or past partner find personalized ways to stay safe and be well.

iHEAL app, "Finding Support For a Safe and Healthy Path Forward," https://ihealapp.ca/en/

FOR MEN

Intimate partner violence against men and boys:

Information and resources for support, validation, advice, and referrals.

Government of Canada, "Intimate Partner Violence Against Men and Boys," Information and Resources, https://www.canada.ca/en/public-health/services/health-promotion/stop-family-violence/intimate-partner-violence-against-men-boys-information-resources.html

SOURCES AND NOTES

THE MAIN SOURCES for this book are the author's own recollections and personal experiences with her family, friends, counsellors, lawyers, the justice system, and the broader public. Transcripts of her interviews with the RCMP and the Mass Casualty Commission are publicly available online through the Commission's records.

Notes

1. Dr. Caroline Fenkle, "Is Fawning a Trauma Response? What You Need to Know," *charliehealth.com*, last updated July 30, 2023, www.charliehealth.com/post/is-fawning-a-trauma-response-what-you-need-to-know.
2. Nova Scotia Government, "First Presumptive Cases of COVID-19 in Nova Scotia; New Prevention Measures," news release, March 15, 2020, *Nova Scotia Department of Health and Wellness COVID-19*, https://news.novascotia.ca/en/2020/03/15/first-presumptive-cases-covid-19-nova-scotia-new-prevention-measures.
3. "Maritime Diefenbunker," *Wikipedia*, last modified July 2021, https://en.wikipedia.org/wiki/CFS_Debert#Maritime_%22Diefenbunker%E2%80%9.
4. The Joint Federal/Provincial Mass Casualty Commission into the April, 2020 Nova Scotia Casualty, "Volume 2: What Happened" in *Turning the Tide Together, Final Report of the Mass Casualty Commission* (His Majesty the King in Right of Canada, 2023), 30, 31, 32, 38, 39, 43, 71, 99, 123,164, 165, 175, 185, 209, https://masscasulatycommission.ca/ and "What Happened – Timeline", at https://timeline.masscasualtycommission.ca.
5. The Joint Federal/Provincial Mass Casualty Commission into the April 2020 Nova Scotia Casualty, "Mass Casualty Exhibit, May 13, 2020 Cst. B MacLeod Description of Events," 5, https://masscasualtycommission.ca/files/fd-source-

materials/COMM0012927.pdf?t=1761430626. "Mass Casualty Exhibit, September 10, 2021 Commission Interview of Cst. Ben MacLeod," https://masscasualtycommission.ca/files/fd-source-materials/COMM0015510.pdf?t=1761430626.

6. The Joint Federal/Provincial Mass Casualty Commission into the April, 2020 Nova Scotia Casualty, "Volume 2: What Happened" in *Turning the Tide Together, Final Report of the Mass Casualty Commission* (His Majesty the King in Right of Canada, 2023), 164,165, 175, 185, 209, 216, 228, 229, 230, 239, 239, https://masscasulatycommission.ca/ and "What Happened – Timeline" at https://timeline.masscasualtycommission.ca.
7. The Joint Federal/Provincial Mass Casualty Commission into the April 2020 Nova Scotia Casualty, "Mass Casualty Exhibit, April 20, 2020: Transcript of Statement by Lisa Banfield taken by Staff Sergeant Vardy," 1–54 https://masscasualtycommission.ca/files/fd-source-materials/COMM0003436.pdf?t=1761480127.
8. CPAC, "RCMP Update on Investigation into Nova Scotia Attacks – April 28, 2020," *YouTube*, April 28, 2020, https://www.youtube.com/results?search_query=Press+Conference+April+28%2C+2020+Darren+Campbell.
9. The Joint Federal/Provincial Mass Casualty Commission into the April 2020 Nova Scotia Casualty, "Mass Casualty Exhibit, April 28, 2020: Transcript of Statement by Lisa Banfield taken by Staff Sergeant Vardy," 1–124, https://masscasualtycommission.ca/files/fd-source-materials/COMM0004070.pdf?t=1761480127.
10. Canadian Red Cross, "Stronger Together Nova Scotia Fund: Update," *Red Cross In Your Community*, April 12, 2020, https://www.redcross.ca/in-your-community/nova-scotia/news-and-stories/stronger-together-nova-scotia-fund-update.
11. The Joint Federal/Provincial Mass Casualty Commission into the April 2020 Nova Scotia Casualty, "Mass Casualty Exhibit, October 23, 2020: Lisa Banfield Video Reenactment with RCMP – Part 4," https://masscasualtycommission.ca/fd-source-videos/COMM0013734/.
12. Royal Canadian Mounted Police—Nova Scotia, "Statement from Supt. Darren Campbell re: H-Strong, December 4, 2020," Public Information Office, rcmpns-grcne@rcmp-grc.gc.ca.
13. Dr. Peter Jaffe, Ph.D., C. Psych., Director Emeritus of the Centre for Research and Education Violence against Women and Children, "Psychological Assessment of Lisa Banfield," January 10, 2022.
14. Tim Bousquet, "The Witchification of Lisa Banfield," *Halifax Examiner*, July 17, 2022.

15. The Joint Federal/Provincial Mass Casualty Commission into the April, 2020 Nova Scotia Casualty, "Executive Summary and Recommendations" in *Turning the Tide Together, Final Report of the Mass Casualty Commission* (His Majesty the King in Right of Canada, 2023), 41, 42, 115, 148, 154–156, 163.

ABOUT THE AUTHORS

LISA BANFIELD grew up in the rural suburban community of Lower Sackville, Nova Scotia. Lisa was the second-youngest of nine children. Her memoir about her harrowing experience as a survivor of intimate partner violence is her first book.

SHERRI AIKENHEAD began her twenty-year journalism career as a writer for *Maclean's* in Toronto. She then worked at the *Edmonton Journal* before returning to Nova Scotia, where she was the managing editor of *The Daily News* in Halifax. Her first book, *Mommy Don't: From Mother to Murder—The True Story of Penny and Karissa Boudreau,* appeared on both the *Globe and Mail* and *Toronto Star* bestseller lists. It was a 2024 finalist for the prestigious Evelyn Richardson Award for Non-Fiction. More information can be found on her website www.sherriaikenhead.com.

MAUREEN BANFIELD is one of Lisa's older sisters, a retired educator with a master's in administrative leadership and counselling. She worked for the Nova Scotia government before the 2020 tragedy. This is her first published collaboration.

ACKNOWLEDGEMENTS

FIRST AND FOREMOST, I would like to thank God for my faith in knowing that with Him and through Him all things are possible.

To my entire "Banfield Clan"—you are a huge part of my life and what I consider to be my greatest blessing. Thank you for loving me through all my life's decisions and most especially the past five years. Your support and unconditional love saved my life. We will heal together, as always.

To the families of all the victims, though this is my story and my perspective, we will forever share unspeakable pain. I pray for God's grace and merciful healing.

To Sherri Aikenhead, co-author: your best-selling expertise crafted my memoir with authentic passion, professionalism, and integrity. Writing about such a serious and sensitive subject requires a special gift that few have; your thoroughness and fierce commitment to the truth speak to your character as an author. Because of your steadfast loyalty and tender approach, you have my lifelong trust and gratitude.

My deepest appreciation to Jo-Anne MacDonald for her copy editing of our initial draft, invaluable insights, and overall encouragement.

To Kenneth Whyte, the owner and publishing executive of Sutherland House: your vision and intentions are pure and made me feel safe in telling my story. Your extraordinary team, Sarah Minaci-Davis, Leah Ciani, and Shalomi Ranasinghe, helped capture my experience for the benefit of so many affected by intimate partner violence. Thank you for your esteemed guidance throughout.

I owe my mental health healing to many professionals. Each of you invested more than your expert talent; your genuine care touched my heart at a time I needed it so desperately. My emotional saviours: Lisa Richardson, Dr. Elaine Davies, and Shireen Singer, you are incredible, professional women who have had a tremendous impact on my healing journey. I am forever grateful.

I am indebted to my justice warriors who fought for me: James Lockyer, Jessica Zita, Peter Rumscheidt, Ian Hull, and Brian Murphy. Thanks to you, I felt protected and heard.

Additionally, I would like to thank those whose compassion superseded their professional role: the Mass Casualty Commission Team including Gillian Hnatiw, Liz Montgomery, Emily Hill, and restorative leaders Jake MacIsaac and Denise Russell. Your collective brilliance and intuitive passion safely navigated me to the other side.

To my dearest friend, Denise: Thank you for helping to put me back together. You are my soul sister for life—from grade school to grave. I love you.

Renée Carston (Baker), you had my back during the most troubling times of my life. You were a safe friend with whom I could confide. I always felt and appreciated your support and love.

To my live-in sissies, Janice and Maureen, you figuratively and literally lifted me up from the darkest time of my life. You advocated and took care of me in every sense of the word. You helped me find my voice again, which led me to find my way back home. I can never express enough the depths of my gratitude and respect. Our bond is unbreakable and our love is eternal.

Maureen: You have always been my rock. You are a significant co-author of my book; because of our blended souls, my voice resonates through your written words. Your faith in me gave me strength to tell my story.

To the many survivors of intimate-partner violence and other loving strangers who extended their hearts through messages of encouragement and hope, I offer my deepest gratitude. We need each other and I will pay forward your kindness, understanding, and love by serving others. We have donated some of the proceeds of this book to transition houses in Nova Scotia.

Lastly, to the readers who chose this book: writing this book has been cathartic and life-changing for me. I pray we all remember that the dark and ugly in this world can always be conquered by humanity's grace as it is inherently divine.

Thank you to all who give voice to truth and light.

GILLIAN HNAT...

...ut, you know, plan...

...nt?

...S. LISA BANFIELD:

...S. GILLIAN HNAT...

...anning to perpetra...

MS. LISA BANFIELD...

MS. GILLIAN HNAT...

...quired an RCMP...